COME SHINING

Come Shining

ESSAYS AND POEMS
ON WRITING IN A DARK TIME

Jill Elliott
Alison Towle Moore
Editors

kelson
books

Portland, Oregon
David Oates, General Editor

Published by Kelson Books

Collection copyright © 2017 by Kelson Books
All contents within are copyright © 2017 by their respective creators.
Cover photo © Horatio Law.

For information please write to kelsonbooks@gmail.com or

Kelson Books
2033 SE Lincoln
Portland OR 97214

The text of this book is set in Arno Pro, a humanistic serif typeface designed by Robert Slimbach and based on 15th- and 16th-century Aldine and Venetian styles.

Printed in the USA

ISBN 978-0-9827838-2-5

Library of Congress Control Number: 2017950539

Contents

III: FINDING OUR WAY FORWARD

The worst is not so long as we can say, 'This is the worst.' Isn't that the truth. Deepstep now baby deepstep. Bear me along your light-bearing paths. Come shining.

– C.D. Wright, *Deepstep Come Shining*

Introduction

DAVID OATES

Sleeplessness ought to be like being awake. But it isn't.

Since November I've been sleepless too often, spent too many before-dawn hours bewildered, angry, fearful, resigned. . . . By what depravity could such an obvious con-man be chosen president? What disregard for mere decency or the simple mental hygiene of truth? What base attraction to swaggering, bullying immaturity – so evident in every utterance, every gesture of this absurd parody of manliness? In the gray hours I try to conceive the inconceivable and fail every time, turning it over and over.

How much company I must have had in these twilight dead-marches! For almost instantly a flood of manifestos and declarations and statements of human values appeared, institutional and individual alike – I saw scores of them, and there must have been hundreds or thousands more. Each of us crying out our No to this ignorant nonsense, and our Yes to each other – ironic validation of community and togetherness, a little too late. And leaving us shocked . . . *shocked!* . . . at the spectacle of organized selfishness and bigotry.

I am old enough not to be surprised. My teen years began precisely, unforgettably, with the assassination of John Kennedy, and were forced to awareness by the murder of Martin Luther King, and ripened horribly through the years of official lying and pointless slaughter achieved by Nixon and his predecessor. Under such tutoring, how could I ever again be surprised at anything?

I should have known better. *Would* have, if I had cared more about those on the margins, for whom none of this was really working. Those were some broad margins, millions deep. But to them I was inattentive, lulled in the pleasant reading of my own life.

My offer to host the *On Writing in a Dark Time* writing group went out in December, and within a week or two, writers had filled every slot. All of us felt that the class was a lifeline, a relief from solitary fears and axe-grinding rants. We needed to understand what was happening to our country. I gathered poems and essays – Hannah Arendt, Václav Havel, W.H. Auden, Adrienne Rich, and many others – to guide our thinking and inspire our writing.

In the darkness, the first rule is to find each other. Meeting together through an unusually stormy Portland winter, we came to see that reading and writing were a virtual commons, a public space where citizenship was reclaimed. We took heart and sharpened our prose. We aimed to write short, to cut deep and speak plain.

We explored difficulty and struggle in many forms: electoral, racial, familial, personal. We began to see that the angry dysfunction of our political moment had its roots in isolation, what Arendt had called simply "loneliness." Displaced or alienated from the public space where democracy thrived, too many citizens had been converted into mere consumers, solitary screen-watchers suddenly given belonging in a fake community of manipulated outrage. Most of all, Arendt taught us the centrality of respect for truth: when that goes, everything goes. In her account of the nineteen-thirties and forties we saw our own country's swerve toward heedless mendacity.

And we have awakened to this: that the struggle is perennial. Our predicament is not some unheard-of aberration, not some unique problem of greedy Republicans or do-gooding liberals or clueless Americans. It is a *human* problem, solved and faced and despaired of uncountable times in the past. T.S. Eliot framed it for us:

> *There is only the fight to recover what has been lost*
> *And found and lost again and again: and now, under conditions*
> *That seem unpropitious . . .*

From Havel we learned to see that hope was a state of mind, a commitment; and that every true word we read or wrote – every word true to life, true to emotion, true to beauty – was an act of resistance, an accession to the strange, subversive power of the powerless. This was revolutionary: an invitation to explore in tenderness as well as outrage. All good work, we discovered, was resistance.

So we resisted, trying to tell truth with love or at least kindness, because we knew (too well!) that humans are fearful and stressed, and it is hard work to care about truth. That's the problem democracy can't quite solve – unless it decides it wants to.

We write to help it decide. Sometimes it works.

When we began to talk about this collection, we knew we wanted to bring in more voices. We sent out a call: *What is this darkness?* And – maybe more important – *What is the quality of light?* We received essays and poems from all over the country. They are gathered into this volume with our own work. We mean this book to mark our moment and to bear witness: this is how it was to watch darkness coming and cry out in opposition. This is how it feels to be human in a dark time.

If we seek truth, it will show us more than we bargain for. For this era of trumpery reveals not just our sad self-involved president's limits and absurdities. If we are shocked and surprised, then such times also illuminate whatever lingering unrealisms had lurked in ourselves – in our progressive program, our liberal project that somehow failed to reckon sufficiently with darkness. So we are called, right now, to this: let us fashion a truer sense of history and a more steely awareness of our kind. Let us make progress, or justice, or community, of that. If we can.

We write in hope. For these dark and unpropitious times also contain miracles of beauty and kindness, spectacles of selflessness, revelations of joy. As all times do. This paradox could point us toward what writing is really for: *to attempt to do justice to all of it.* All of it: this glorious misery, this shared loneliness, this collective search for the means and the courage to live in truth.

We welcome our readers to this confused condition. We wish them light and awakening in this struggle.

In solidarity,

David Oates
August 2017
Portland

I

FACING THE DARKNESS

Americans at Sea

TINA TAU

"All Americans are loud," says Thijs. He is Dutch. We are both practicing knots in the deckhouse.

"All Americans?" I don't think I'm loud. I want him to exempt me.

"All of them." His voice is firm. I am interested. Not offended. Puzzled.

There are five Americans on board the tall ship *Europa*. The other forty-five are Europeans and Australians. We are all "crew," but thirty-one of us have paid for the adventure of sailing across the Atlantic, while nineteen sunburned, skilled people are working for pay. I got on in the sun-sweet Canary Islands, and I'm disembarking in Uruguay, after a month and a half at sea. Most of the voyage crew have sailed some kind of boat before, but I've never climbed into rigging or hauled a line or steered a course in my life.

Some Americans are loud, I grant you that. Mike has a voice that will drop you to the floor. He's a retired New Jersey cop. Tall, crew-cut, back-slapping friendly. His opinions are heavy. "You could throw a dart into the ocean and whatever you hit would be a better candidate than either of those two idiots," he growls during our first conversation at the helm, in October.

Every morning Elliott or someone from the permanent crew gives a lecture: about the mizzenmast, or the three kinds of north, or how to use a sextant. Elliott also says that anyone on the voyage crew can give a talk if they want to.

I step right up and give the first talk. It's on dreams. My goal is to get people to tell me their dreams, so I will have a role on this boat besides smiling and standing lookout. As the oldest woman aboard (by far) and a non-sailor, I fear no one will know who I really am.

A week later, Bill gives a talk about being a Mormon. None of the Europeans has met an actual Mormon before, and they are curious. I know Mormons but in fact his talk is helpful and strange. It turns out that he believes in the literal truth of the Bible; the world was created in six days and all that. Bill looks like Santa Claus and is just as nice. I am startled to discover what he actually thinks.

Mike calls his lecture: "Everything you ever wanted to ask a cop but were afraid to ask." I slide into a seat in the deckhouse just as Nellie, a funny, clear-headed Australian, asks Mike a pointed question about guns. He explains that all gun control would do is keep the good guys from defending themselves, because the bad guys get their guns illegally anyway. He's so sure about this that he is not even defensive. I look around; the Europeans are watching him, mouths zipped.

After Mike's talk, I stand out on the deck with Victoria, a shy nurse from Sweden. The deck boards are warm on my bare feet. The sky is luminous, the sails white and taut, the sea bluer and even more luminous than the sky. We are in the silent, wind-driven lap of the world.

Victoria says, "I'm afraid to go to America."

"Oh, it's not as bad as you think." I look into her earnest eyes. "Most gun violence happens between people who know each other. Not to tourists. And really, the worst of it is in the South. I don't worry about gun violence in my everyday life, you know." My stomach is tense. Why am I saying this? As if I didn't want to wail and hide my head. *Me too! I'm afraid to go to America!* But I give her a reassuring smile.

In any community of fifty people, there will be some great storytellers. It's true on this narrow blade of a ship. Amber is a twenty-three-year-old Australian military diplomat, Mick a career oil tanker captain, Bianca an international aid worker in Nepal. We have adventurers, soldiers, a man who rescued hundreds of wild animals.

But none of those people give a talk. The three of us who do are all, hm, Americans. We stand up and tell everybody what we think, what we believe, what is important to us. *Loud* might not be exactly the right word, but Thijs was onto us. We take up more than our share of space. I am sad, as I realize this tree has its roots in me too.

We are almost to Uruguay when the results of the American election slug me in the chest. I cry in the breakfast room, and Nellie puts her arms around me. Once again, I'm embarrassed to be an American, and now I feel sick. I know the world is watching, and in many ways it has its arms around us. We are all in this together, one world – right here by the oatmeal –

And yet. . .

Election Results, By State

JEREMY CANTOR

A wants me dead and says so.
B wants me dead, but will not say so
until he hears *A* say so.
C wants me dead but will never say so,
though he'll gladly vote for that result.
D wants me dead but says he doesn't.
E does not want me dead but
is willing for me to be killed if
that will get him what he wants.
F does not want me dead but
is willing for me to be killed
because *A, B, C, D*, and *E* have
told him that it will get him what he wants,
though it isn't true.
G doesn't care one way or the other
but is scared of *A, B, C, D* and *F*.
H doesn't want me dead but is
scared of *A, B, C, D* and *F* and is

disappointed by **G**.
And *I* don't know what I should do.

(The American press calls that
"*a polarized electorate.*")

The Catkins Burst on Their Own

JOHN BRANTINGHAM

Annie and I stand on the edge of Cahoon Meadow just a few miles into the backcountry talking about catkins, the way they explode into a kind of green fog of pollen around a pine tree when they reach the right temperature. The tree gets fuzzy for a moment and then the powder reshapes itself to fit the wind currents around it.

I nod to the cloud. "I must be slowing down or something," I say to Annie. "This is the first year I've ever noticed that."

"Nah," she says. "This is just the first time you've lived like this."

She's right. It's been five weeks that we've been off grid and living in a tent. I've started to see the place in a way that I never would have before. Even in the forest, I would have been thinking about the emails that I need to send out or something I'd seen on television. Instead, I sit here watching the nature's summer and working my way out of thought.

In a while, we start down the path. It's been a long hike today, but not a hard one. We woke before the sun, and it's still early. I don't know what time it is, and I don't care. To get down off this part of the mountain, we have to go down a long flight of stairs that someone carved into the rocks maybe fifty or a hundred years ago, and coming down, we meet a couple who look college age coming up.

We step out of the way to let them pass, but they pause where they are, panting from the climb. The woman out of breath groans. The man laughs, "Don't worry about her," he says. "She's just not used to walking this far without capturing a Pokémon."

It seems like a snippy kind of comment, and I'm expecting some kind of fight to break out here, but she leans on her walking stick and laughs. "He's not wrong, you know. I don't suppose you can catch a signal up there." She nods the way Annie and I have come.

I turn to Annie, but she just shrugs. "I'm sorry," I say, "but I don't know what you're talking about."

She explains it to me. Apparently, in the last five weeks, the cyber world has figured out a way to force people to leave their houses chasing after Pokémon with cell phones. It's a global phenomenon the man tells me. Everyone in the world is doing it. Even his mother is doing it, and he names her age, which is younger than mine.

The young woman explains the game, and it sounds like a lot of fun. If I had a cell phone, which I don't, and lived within a signal, which I also don't, I would certainly be joining in. It's a rare time in our modern world when everyone is sharing an experience and finding joy. I try to remember another similar instance and can only come up with the moon landing.

Everyone in the world is playing this game, I think, except Annie and me. We are certainly missing out. There is value in joining in with that kind of global phenomenon, but there is value in missing it as well.

We sit down on these stairs to catch up on so much that we have missed. People have been killed in France while celebrating Bastille Day. Gay men have been murdered in a nightclub by a homophobic psychopath. Black men have been killed in their cars with no real provocation, and police officers have been ambushed in a flimsy excuse for retribution for those killings. The election goes on, they tell us, and the Olympics are coming up too, Zika virus or not.

Eventually, we all decide to push off. They have miles to go into their world of natural isolation, and I wish I were off with them. We're coming back to our base camp, which bumps into the other world every once in a while. "It's enough to make you forget about the catkins," I say.

"Nah," Annie says. "This isn't anything new."

She's right. It's chaos off the mountain, but when is it not? The giant pine trees that we've been watching this afternoon are old enough to have lived through World War II, Andrew Jackson, and Napoleon's hundred days. They've seen the moon landing too, and all of the modern Olympics. Nations come and go. Peace has been created and destroyed, but in that time, the temperature has gotten to be just warm enough every summer that the catkins have exploded the pollen into Cahoon Meadow. Sometimes people have seen it and sometimes not, but this year, we are here.

In a couple of months, I might be chasing Pokémon through the streets of Los Angeles, and I certainly will be voting, but at this moment, all I am is here.

Trauma, On Repeat

ANDY SMART

The day my father shot himself, my mother looked at me with a vacancy I didn't know was possible.

"I can't believe he did this to us," she said. And she kept saying it. She'd remind the air around her that she was stunned. That this reality was too much for her, too absurdly traumatic. It made it even difficult to grieve, the strangeness of the fact of Dad's suicide.

That day, June 15, 2007, was the worst day of my life. I'm sure that makes me selfish – 9/11 should probably eclipse my personal tragedy because of its scope, its historical significance, and its continuing reverberation. But my dad deciding to put a gun in his mouth was worse than that and it sets the bar, I hope, too high for any terror to surmount.

But any agony is open to being echoed.

Election night, 2016: Mom and I are at Heavy Anchor, our favorite bar in St. Louis. We're surrounded by friends wearing "Feel the Bern" shirts and "I'm With Her" pins, strangers with

"Fuck Trump" fake tattoos on their cheeks, and a couple of corgis with no stake in the results.

"You're going to see the first woman President," I say.

"I think so, too," Mom says.

She has come into herself since my father's death. Become a short-haired, born-again feminist half-hippie. She dreams aloud of seeing the glass ceiling made into shrapnel by the ascent of Hillary Rodham Clinton. Her hope is written in her posture and the nervous way she sips her Diet Coke. When Dad was alive, Mom would never have been out this late – in a tavern talking politics with her gay Guatemalan friend Danny, no less. And she wouldn't have been such an outspoken supporter of a female candidate.

It's hard for a son to see his father's shadow as a weight oppressing his mother. But it's a proper misery for that son to watch his mother witness the election of Donald Trump.

Reddening states on a virtual map. That's how we knew. It wasn't a pool of blood, but it was. It was the arterial spray from a wound to my mother's United States. Texts started coming from absentee friends.

Surreal, maybe, would be the word. A nauseous farcical dream we'd all wake up from. When my father died, the overarching sentiment, even outside the family, was: *there's just no way*. And here tonight it was the same.

Just before last call, Mom's mantra of yesteryear is reborn with a timely mutation: "I can't believe they did this to us."

They. The percentage of our co-citizens who elected Trump. The opposition. I try not to surrender to the sociological bifurcation. I try; I fail. I am at odds with my neighbors as I was once at odds with my father's ghost. The stitches are torn from the wound. A weird fever of infection threatens.

"I can't believe it either," I say. "I can't believe what they've done."

Six months after Dad's death, Mom and I went to a support group. Something about sitting in a circle of folks with similar damage sounded useful. Together we'd talk through the agonies and loneliness, the abandonment. The disbelief. We'd reconcile the seeming irrationality of our loved ones actions to some kind of logic. Some truth deeper than the knowable.

So every Tuesday for a year we went. We began each meeting by stating our individual facts: who died, when, method of choice, their age at the time. After that, we'd share.

"How are you feeling?" the moderator would ask.

"Angry. Confused. Mostly angry," I'd say.

That concise rage would last me five years.

"I stayed in bed all day today," Mom says into the phone.

"I thought you might," I say.

The election is not twenty-four hours past but we have both aged. Our country has morphed into a Faulkner-esque landscape; we, like the characters in *The Sound and the Fury*, are all clamoring to make sense of our environs. We are, like Benjy Compson, "trying to say."

"The Trumpers are unbearable," Mom says. "The things they're saying about us. About Hillary. I can't believe we live around the corner from these people."

"I know. It's like I know a bunch of closet Nazis and Trump is the door. Now everything hateful, abstruse, unfounded, or spiteful is okay to say."

"But it's not though," she says. "It's not."

Eventually, the support group dissolved and Mom and I were alone with Dad's death. We lived together with our separate burdens. For her, it was quietude that soothed. But I needed something tangible. Not a coping device, but a product of recovery. Something to prove I was being okay.

I went back to school for English under the pretense of honoring a promise to Dad. And I started to write. The first syllable about my old man was more monumental than any grief or rage I'd known. It echoed over the tiny rooftops of what I wanted to say and came back to me, hard. They were ugly, the first attempts at making art out of ashes and vitriol. So began my slow divorce from my anger, the fresh burns we suffer when fleeing a burning house.

When the beginning was over, I had a poem.

I send a letter to poet Bruce Weigl in Lorrain, Ohio, who is known for his writing in his own dark time, Vietnam. The let-

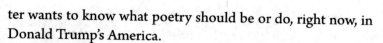

ter wants to know what poetry should be or do, right now, in Donald Trump's America.

"Good question," Bruce replies. "I don't think satire . . . or clever iambic pentameter are the answer, though."

Bruce tells me what we both know: that Trump threatens to defund the Arts and that we should unite to keep creative pursuits relevant. It's too grand a mission for the moment, for me.

"Send me a poem," Bruce says.

There are plenty of online communities for artists against Donald Trump. Plenty of magazines and blogs seeking poetry and prose in response to the political weather. But there is only one Bruce, and one me – only one correspondence that will make a shared memory.

A Cuban woman lives six blocks from my house in a four-family flat. I said good morning to her in Spanish last week and she giggled. I learned to say "God be with you" in Gaelic because there are Irish interns in the hotel where I work. And I wrote a poem for Bruce Weigl at lunch this afternoon.

Posterity is vast and distant. To say we should make beauty and be beautiful so that we might be remembered well is foolish. But to say that the simple language of being human may etch a portrait of us in the breathing history of our neighbors is not. Faced with a grandiloquently bigoted leadership, being a soothing phrase or a whisper of truth is not only an art but a mission. To say a thing which needs to be heard and to say it well and often. To commune with one another in something other than celebration of the cheap thrill of breathing.

Silence is not only unpleasant and dishonest. It's dangerous. Let us always be "trying to say."

My father lived Thoreau's trope – a life of quiet desperation. Only in its end and aftermath was Dad's existence loud.

We are and should be sound. Fury. I say preempt the echo.

On Celebrating a Birthday the Same Day as a New U.S. President is Inaugurated

HEIDI BEIERLE

A snowy mountain of whipped cream sparkling with sugar crystals stands firmly in a serving bowl, centerpiece for the waffle topping station in Timberline Lodge's dining room. I'm overnighting here on Mt. Hood with a good friend as part of my birthday celebration. I dig with a serving spoon three times into the mountain of cream, carving a chasm in its slope, and let the cream fall in dollops into my cup-sized bowl. I speckle the stiff peaks with mini chocolate chips.

Back at my sturdy wooden seat, I spoon small bites of the sweet cream and chocolate into my mouth. Face down on the table next to me, my phone buzzes with Facebook notifications. I don't want to look. I don't want to see posts about the catastrophe upon us because the new President is taking office, and I certainly don't want to see this invective tagged on with birthday greetings. With all the political chatter around me on Facebook, I feel judged. I wonder, *How can you possibly celebrate today?* Steering away from that seems like a hell of a good reason to not be on Facebook. Yet, I like happy birthday wishes.

The buttery cream melts over my tongue, and I crush the chocolate between my molars to scatter its bitterness, fat mingling with fat.

Fat. What a word. Fat. Fat. Fat.

No amount of repeating the word makes me feel any more comfortable with how it's used, even as I delight in its richness coating my tongue. As nutritional descriptor, it's judged and steeped in shame – good fat, bad fat. I turn my head as if that will protect me from the hurt unleashed from mentally mouthing this F-word.

Fat makes me uncomfortable – in my clothes, in my psyche, in front of the mirror, on my plate, in someone else's mouth. In this moment though, the birthday party is in my mouth. This bowl of whipped cream and chocolate isn't the only thing I've eaten for breakfast today, but I allowed myself this indulgence to mark my forty-second birthday. And I'm enjoying it despite myself, despite my country, and despite what feels like the world around me pressing in like a murder of crows.

I was born on January twentieth, although no U.S. President was inaugurated in 1975.

Born in the heart of winter, my birthday always has more darkness than light.

This last year has been fraught with personal challenges: divorce, losing my job, starting a business, breaking a bone, losing another job. I've wanted answers. Why am I the person these things happen to? Why are things so difficult? What am I supposed to be doing with my life?

On New Year's Day, I went to a morning yoga class. I wondered if going to class would help me feel better about the fat I accumulated over the fall and winter. And, if not feel better accepting my fat, I guessed I would certainly feel better exercising to make it go away.

Special for New Year's Day, the teacher made crème brulée, which she invited all the students to have. A cup of cream was the last thing I needed, but my belly was willing to receive this lesson.

"First, have some pickled ginger and turmeric," the teacher instructed, "to aid digestion. Then have the crème brulée. The fat from the cream will fuel you to digest the rest of your meal."

I couldn't believe my ears. Even though she had also made brunch to share with us, she wanted us to have dessert first. Inside, I heard chanting as if my belly were at a rally: Dessert first! Dessert first! And then my mind took over. Would it fill me up? Would I want another?

I'd like to say I ate the entire thing mindfully, but I didn't. Within a minute, I sat with an empty ramekin in one hand and a spoon licked shiny in the other.

"It's ok to eat crème brulée every day," the teacher said. Well, that's what I heard her say.

I traded my ramekin for a paper plate of lentils and rice and sat in an open chair next to a woman named Pat. We made small talk, during which I told her about the consulting business I had started and described my specialty area in active travel options. She wanted to know how I got interested in this career field.

It wasn't easy to answer. Whatever clarity I seemed to have gained in the last year to pursue this work perched on an iceberg of confusion.

Something I said prompted her to ask, "Is there a relationship involved?"

"Yes and no," I said. "I returned to yoga after nine years away to help recover from divorce. Crafting my work and discovering where to go with my life is part of the process."

"That might be where I'm headed," she said.

"Are you divorced?" I asked.

"I'm trying to sort that out," she said. "You seem like you know where you're going." She looked at me as if I could throw her a life preserver.

"I don't have any answers," I told her and then almost chortled, "except there are no answers." I put my hand on her arm. I hadn't expected how unnerving saying that would feel. While I thought the gesture was to reassure her, it seemed to be for me. I felt less scared in the face of Vast, Answerless Uncertainty by touching her. "Yoga helps," I said. "It gives me tools to find balance when I'm dying for an answer and there isn't one."

I spoon another bite of whipped cream into my mouth. The fat and sugar slither across my tongue. The administration change in the White House amplifies my awareness of the Unknown as I acknowledge it does for so many other people. I'm interested in what this dark specter of change has to teach me. Does it obscure truth or invite me to encounter it? If, like the fat I eat, I can accept the unseemly heaviness as part of who I am, will I taste liberty?

Election Results, By County

JEREMY CANTOR

The meanest boy on the playground
meandered in my general direction,
demonstrating just for me that he
was in no hurry, maintaining an eye-lock
so that I could not possibly mistake his intent,
so he could enjoy my fear to the fullest.
He was the boy who was famous for stealing
everybody's lunch money, and now that same everybody
was patting him on the back as they passed
with an "attaboy!" as he drew his switchblade
from his pocket, his eyes never leaving mine even
as he flicked it open and they all murmured what
a great guy he was and they would always
be right behind him because he had
promised to buy them lunch.

A Family History of Distortion

BESS BACALL

My family has a genius for erasing reality. You could describe my life as one long lesson in learning to ignore the glittery mirage and focus instead on the harsh, windy desert.

If you asked my father, he would have told you that economic security was what he valued most. His father had fled to New York to escape conscription in the Czar's army. He was paid in liquor and herring for factory work; he drank the liquor and spilled the herring.

After the war, my father became a CPA. His bad temper and undisguised contempt for his superiors cost him a string of jobs, but he was convinced that he had a 'feel' for the market and could make a living trading. His radio was always tuned to market reports: the Dow up a half, NASDAQ down three-quarters. He talked more to his broker than his wife or kids, and still he lost money. We lived on my mother's salary as a teacher. At the end of his life, my father's estate was a Dixie cup half-full of change from the penny poker game at the Rose Schnitzer Manor.

If you asked my mother, she would tell you that family is what she values most. She married at twenty-one, but the marriage was troubled from the start, and my parents did not try to hide their unhappiness.

The summer I was six, the Alice Crimmins case hit the front pages of all the New York papers. Alice Crimmins was twenty-six, red-headed, busty, and skilled with the eyeliner and teasing comb. My mother envied Alice's figure but thought she looked "hard."

Alice's marriage was on the rocks. Her husband claimed she was an unfit mother and sought custody of their two children, but they remained with her during the separation. On the morning of July 15, 1965, Alice called her husband and accused him of taking the children from her home. Later that day, the corpse of Missy, their five-year-old daughter, was found in a vacant lot a few blocks from the family home. A few days later, the body of their son Eddie, six like me, turned up where it had been dumped on the weedy shoulder of the VanWyck Expressway. The Queens D.A. charged Alice with murder. Her motive was to clear the way for a new boyfriend, a millionaire contractor.

The legal proceedings dragged on into the early nineteen-seventies, when I was in junior high. I don't remember exactly when my mother, a member of the National Organization of Women and fervently pro-choice, told me that Alice Crimmins was her hero. She explained that, from a feminist perspective, a woman's right to choose should extend until her children were viable, meaning that they could survive on their own. She said that the age of viability varied, but that in New York City, with the cost of living as high as it was, a child would not be truly viable until the age of sixteen.

Understanding that I was holding her back from the life she wanted, I worked hard to justify my existence. I wrote her poems, bought her gifts, and served as her loyal and steadfast confidante. Of course nothing I did was ever enough. As her demands on me increased, I dreamed of the time I would be old enough to move away.

So Donald Trump is not news to me. The fictions, the vanity, the selfishness. The alternative facts. The front page of the New York Times shows him at his desk in the Oval Office, the Leader of the Free World. The deckle-edged photographs in my mother's old navy blue album show a happy family. I know how to correct for reality, but it is exhausting, and it stirs up old grief.

As a child, I believed my parents were not interested in me because I was bad, and tried to convince them that I was worthy of love. Now I know my hypothesis was wrong. The worlds they inhabited had nothing to do with me, or anything else occupying the present moment. The engines that powered their fantasies were built long ago, in their childhoods, and were beyond reach. I think this is true of our president, whose father, Fred Trump, was by all accounts a stern master of conditional love. What is happening now, in some awful way, has nothing to do with us at all.

Setting boundaries on the attention I give my mother, who has a bottomless desire for it, is a continuing struggle. Successes are temporary. Containing the narcissist is hard, often exhausting work. But recovering one's self is even harder.

I am an expert on my mother's feelings, but hardly know my own. I can describe her ambitions, achieved and thwarted, but struggle to know what I want for dinner, or how I want to spend my time on a holiday weekend. When asked a bigger question, like what mark I want to make on the world, I freeze up, flushed with shame. I should know by now, but I don't. The process of recovery requires me to attend to my own infant psyche, to nurture what is there with patience and compassion in the hope that it may yet flower.

The psychotherapist Daniel Shaw says that the relationship between cult leader and acolyte is similar to the one between narcissistic parent and child. The forty-fifth president has much of our nation in his thrall. Like it or not, he is omnipresent, intrusive. He tells us that we are stupid, that our institutions are worthless, that our generosity has made us an easy mark for other nations. When he says we cannot live without his protection, I recognize the falsehood. I have heard it before.

These messages are insidious and destructive. But if, somehow, our press remains independent, and our courts enforce the Constitution, we will eventually be left to carry on.

We have serious work to do. The American idea that each of us is endowed with "an unalienable right to life, liberty, and the pursuit of happiness" still resonates with me, even though I know the signers of the Declaration of Independence had only white male property-owners in mind. Our real history falls short of the myth in so many ways.

But then, my experience of family also fell short of the myth. That hasn't stopped me from trying to create the family that I want. My kids know that I love being their mother. A few years ago, when my teenage daughter was going through a difficult time, I told the man I was dating that I would no longer be available on Friday nights; I wanted to spend that time on the couch with her, eating take-out, debriefing the week, massaging her feet while we watched Project Runway. He did not understand, but my priorities were clear.

Now, I am trying to create the America I want. It's far from an original vision; I learned it before I was ten from my elementary school teachers, in the songs they taught us for assembly: Katherine Howe's "America the Beautiful," Woody Guthrie's "This Land is Your Land," Pete Seeger and Lee Hays' "If I Had a Hammer." Its symbol is more than 125 years old: the Statue of Liberty, the civic goddess who stands in New York Harbor to fulfill the ancient obligation of welcoming the stranger. At her feet are the broken shackles of oppression and tyranny.

This America is a sanctuary for immigrants and refugees. This America is built around abundance, generosity, hard work and innovation. All of us have good healthcare, enough to eat, and safe, stable homes. Everyone is educated to their potential.

I wish I knew for sure how to get from here to there, how to get rid of our racial caste system, our easy violence, and our urban-rural divide. We do not choose our national legacy, any more than we choose our parents. But I have to believe we can choose our future.

> *It's been a long, a long time coming*
> *But I know a change is gonna come, oh yes it will*
> *– Sam Cooke*

The Weight of Lies

KAMALA BREMER

The upstairs loft of the Bombay Cricket Club restaurant was dry and cozy for a wet April night in 2001. The four of us were seated at a square table with a starched white cloth, me, my husband Les, and my good friend Emma with her husband James. This would be our first dinner out together, as the span between our childless fifties and their new parenthood had stood in the way.

Appetizers came, then dinner, along with amusing chatter. Over a second round of mango margaritas, Emma leaned close, suddenly serious, pale eyebrows drawn tight. "You won't believe this. Did you know the Apollo 11 moon landing was faked!"

"What?" I said, momentarily confused, then burst out laughing. "You're joking. Right?" On summer break from college in 1969, I had watched TV coverage of the mission with my parents when Emma and James would have been toddlers. I heard stations across the globe track the capsule's historic journey, pored over *LIFE* magazine's special edition with its amazing color photos of the first humans on the moon.

"No, no, it's true!" Emma insisted. "We grew up believing the Apollo missions were real. But now they say we've been lied to all these years. After the program, James and I held each other and cried all night."

The distance across the table widened as they cited evidence from the show, a "documentary" that had just aired on Fox TV. "Like, they had official film clips of an American flag flying, but everyone knows there's no wind on the moon!"

I scrambled through memory for facts that would verify the mission happened and calm her worry. "There isn't even *air* on the moon. I read about how NASA anticipated that problem, and used a wire frame to make the flag display."

"Besides, that would be one heck of a conspiracy," Les added. "It would have involved tens of thousands of people, including the Russians, who had telemetry as good as ours and tracked every move we made."

After a dozen cycles of supposed evidence and our defense, Emma was near tears. "They even interviewed an astronaut's wife, whose husband had died on the launch pad. Why would she lie?"

I didn't know what to say. It seemed impossible to me that a TV network would purposefully deceive people, plant doubt in their hearts, take away their trust. Even for ratings. Even Fox.

Les interrupted. "Say, do either of you remember that movie about a Mars landing hoax?"

"Capricorn One," James replied. "Came out in the late '70s, I think."

"Twenty-some years ago, but maybe Fox based this new TV show on that idea?" Les dropped the idea on the table, nudged my knee for me to remain quiet, and waited.

After a while, James looked at us soberly. "So basically, you believe we've been duped."

A heaviness I didn't know I was holding lifted from my chest. He was coming around. "Yes, yes, exactly!"

But as we said quick goodbyes on the wet Portland street, I felt like we'd ended the night on different planets, mine with too little gravity, my thoughts spinning wildly. Emma and I had written together for years, sharing words from our deepest souls. How could she, an educated liberal Portlander, have been taken in? But that night must have felt heavy to them. Soon Emma no longer had time for a friendship. We never socialized again.

If that conversation happened today, I like to think I'd be gentler, try to understand why the broadcast affected Emma so strongly, why she'd exchanged belief in our shared reality for doubt and mistrust. But I feel I should still let her know she'd been misled. Recent spacecraft observations show flags from every moon landing still standing, except Apollo 11's flag which toppled during lift-off. Yet Fox TV's stunt helped create an enduring belief by up to 20% of Americans that the moon landings were faked.

At the time, Emma couldn't have expected to see a lie dressed up as a documentary. Neither could I. With my Walter Cronkite-era faith in the media, I didn't even have a name for that kind of lying. But in the years since, outrageous falsehoods have proliferated extensively through social and fringe media, almost becoming a new norm.

My throat aches with the need to shout that enough is enough, this kind of lying needs to stop. It undercuts our shared reality, fragments our culture, sows suspicion and separation. I struggle to understand why this is happening so much now. We've always called things *true* which can be proved by direct observation or a preponderance of hard evidence. And used *opinion* to mean something we believe but can't prove. *Mistaken*, for something a person unwittingly gets wrong, *Lies*, for deliberate falsehoods. None of these described the betrayal I've felt.

But when I read Holocaust refugee Hannah Arendt, who analyzed the politics of WWII and the Vietnam era, I understood that what we see now is not lying as a cover-up, or as sensationalism for profit, but purposeful, structured deceit. Arendt coined the term *organized lying* to mean "mass manipulation of fact and opinion, rewriting history" and changing the "facts" upon which future actions will be based. "Modern political lies are so big," she said, "they require . . . the making of another reality . . . into which they will fit."

These days we hear planned, organized lies erupt from the mouths of right-wing think tanks, talk show hosts, members of Congress, and now the President as well. Arendt summarized the effect: "The result of a consistent and total substitution of lies for factual truth is . . . that the sense by which we take our bearings in the real world . . . is being destroyed." And so the bedrock of truth, on which we can work together and make good decisions, crumbles beneath our feet.

The events of that evening still trouble me, and I miss my friend Emma. I wonder, what will be crushed under the weight of lies in our country now?

Now, at the year's dark cusp,

ELEANOR BERRY

call up the bright bristling, mid-March,
of a swampy thicket on the verge

of budding out, vivid green of rain-
plumped moss setting off
a ruddy haze of branchwork.

Summon all that stirs within
the brimful beaver pond, where
a single heron waits, looking

both sides at once without
the slightest shift in stance.
Imagine all the light

the heron's hungry eyes
gather from water and from sky.

Behind the Sadness
Is the Next Good Idea

SONYA HUBER

Dear Me,

I wanted to remind you that given the state of the nation and government, it's totally normal to be super-depressed. The daily assaults on reason, fact, morality, and the future itself all seem to require a candle lit in the house of mourning. And you – while making your calls and going to rallies – have lit quite a few of those candles.

I mean, really, how could you not? You are technically a clinically depressed person – which always shocks those who see you as super-happy. They don't see that happiness and joy-seeking can be athletically honed and deployed in a systematic way over years and decades until the act of enthusiasm itself – especially in public – is like an outer ear, stretched to collect and amplify joy.

So you have your public enthusiasm, which exists around you like the rings of Saturn, as much to keep people away and keep yourself hidden as anything else. You have your meds (glory be). And you'd upped them even before the election. You already know all the things: exercise, going to meetings and rallies and seeing people, taking breaks. I am not telling you anything you don't already know. So ignore that.

What I want to say is that every few days, you dip into bleakness. And while the bleakness has taken various forms throughout your life, I want to applaud your ability to function. You're still making lists and getting things done. But we have to air out your vices in order to examine them, too. We need to be honest about your penchant, this time around, for stockpiling in small but noticeable amounts, items you think might be necessary after a societal collapse: canned goods (but not enough to actually keep a family alive for an extended period); the crank-operated radio and cell-phone charger (good, but you're assuming there would still be a signal); cash (and as your husband wisely noted, $200 will not get you far). These are nods in the right direction and also candles of mourning.

You have noted that these actions, as ridiculous as they are, improve your mood and overall functioning, so you do them for that very reason if nothing else. And that in itself is wise. Keep making gestures toward an apocalypse you would probably not be very comfortable in because the meds would also run out. And then.

Let's draw back from the apocalypse, even though it's there in your mind's eye. The other object in your house of mourning is shame over the sadness itself and a sense that if you admit it – not your general depression but the monolithic orange obelisk of this specific mourning – you would be draining the movement of energy it needs to continue.

You are putting yourself in a 1960s-era Maoist self-criticism circle of one, decrying your lack of revolutionary commitment because you sometimes get sad. And that, my dear, is the wrong view.

Occasionally, like a lucky penny on the ground, you run into your own sense, which glints in the light of the candles of mourning. Your sense says: you have to feel the feelings, and then behind the feeling is the intelligence and the insight. You can't go around them.

And if you go into the place where dread lives, you see how familiar it still is. In fact you laugh because the furniture is all the same furniture you remember, and you remember hanging those curtains. What is scary about the dread is that it brings up the dread-eras of your life. Yes, this little closet of dread still has your old mix-tapes in a shoe-box near the tape player. Yes, it has your journals in it, and it has wisps of your long hair the last time you grew it as a curtain to hide behind. The apartment of dread smells like cold, but it's the cold you know, almost metallic, and you know where the thermostat is, and you are comforted by the baseboard heaters as they tick and work.

What you find in the apartment of dread with all of your old selves is that the decades you've been alive, with your focused enthusiasm and the conscious construction of days, have built a sturdier sub-floor. You don't even feel like crying much in this apartment. You're scared to be back here, but then is not now.

What's more – and pay attention to this – is that you know very well how to operate in this apartment, from this home base. It's nothing surprising. You can very quickly shove a few new books onto the shelves and set up a command center. You can send out an email – yes, email exists now, though the apartment of dread pre-dates it – that says, oops, I'll be a few days late with this reply.

In fact, you can demand that everyone give everyone else a few days' more leeway with things. Where was that report for work? I must have left it in my dread apartment. We must all be a little more forgiving now.

Your work – and it is good work indeed – is to know that you function well in this universe. And functioning well can sometimes look like crying, and it can sometimes look like needing a night to recover. And it can sometimes look like foggy-head.

Being sad is not a mark of radical insufficiency.

Being sad won't bring other people down.

Being sad is one rational response to our situation.

Being sad needs to take the space it needs or it will take all the space.

Being sad is the work we need to do to get to the other work.

There, behind the sad, is the next good idea.

Love,
Me

II

REFLECTION IN THE DARK

In the Raw

MARIA JAMES-THIAW

I sink to the bottom of a gold rimmed coffee mug.
  I'm the raw sugar that won't dissolve,
  the clump of honey that sticks to the spoon,
the unground bean that somehow got through.
  White sugar melts into the Americano,
  but not me, in the raw.

This place is the cornerstone of this
  once-white town where
  we gather for lattes, lunch, light conversation.
  Aretha's voice is a massage for my soul
  but she sings too soft to drown out
  three generations of mean girls that surround me.

The moms in the front corner,
  with their Tupperware talk,
  the cheerleader chatter in the back,
  and beside my table,

three elderly women –
including the one that
touched my twisted locs
when we were in line –
discuss August Wilson at the Gamut,
and a remake of
"The Birth of a Nation."
It's February.
They'll try to cleanse past sins at the theater.

A cheerleader, skin like espresso, has glued
    an Indian's hair to her scalp.
    She's the cocoa version of her friends.
    I expect a soft smile, a sign that we are linked,
    not isolated, not alone; She offers a
    silky straight hair flip instead.

She's just trying to be sugar –
    trying to dissolve into a boiling hot cup.

Fearful Inheritance

ALISON TOWLE MOORE

I grew up hearing stories from my parents about racism in the Deep South during their early married years. One night in Alabama my father was driving our black housekeeper Lilly home and was pulled over by a pair of white deputies and asked, "What's that nigger doing riding in the front seat?" My dad, in his MP uniform with his own gun visible said, "I'm giving her a ride home and she'll sit where she wants to sit." Someone else might have been shot.

As an Army family we moved nearly every year. I was born in 1961 in Fort Benning, Georgia, the youngest of three daughters. My parents came from New Jersey, my mother's parents immigrants from Glasgow and my father's second-generation Catholic American by way of Ireland and England. John F. Kennedy was their hero. My mother Norma even looked a bit like Jackie, with her high cheekbones and dark bouffant.

Mom shared another story only toward the end of her life. She told me that after a barbecue on a hot summer evening when the kids had been put to bed she and my dad stayed up drinking beer with the neighbors. We lived off base that year in Louisiana. My mother spoke in a low voice and avoided my eyes as she recalled the neighbor, a local man, telling hunting stories. "As he went on," she told me, her voice almost a whisper, "I realized he was talking about hunting black men, about shooting them in the back as they ran." Her body shuddered at the memory.

By 1972 we lived in Alexandria, Virginia when my father left the Pentagon for a second tour of duty in Viet Nam. My mother got a job as a legal secretary to buy me the horse I was desperate for. She had stopped for cigarettes one day and spotted me reading *Mad* magazines and flirting with an older boy at the 7-Eleven on Fort Hunt Road. She decided I needed a focus for my restless, rebellious energy before I started getting into real trouble.

My oldest sister Kath owned a bay gelding named Jeremy. I got a young quarter horse named Lady with little training and a fiery temper like mine. I pedaled my bike hard the two miles each way on narrow hilly roads to Briary Farm where we boarded our horses. Lady and the barn became my life. The huge farm sat west of a middle-class neighborhood of colonial style houses, the Regional Library and Stephen Foster Intermediate School. To the north it abutted Gum Springs, a much poorer black community.

In contrast to our neat subdivision, Gum Springs was full of old shacks. Many had generations of cars in the front yard, the old ones rusting quietly while the newest (usually a Cadillac) took pride of place. My father also had an affinity for Caddies. We called his El Dorado the Brown Turd. I rode Lady many afternoons to the northern corner of Briary Farm where I tethered her to a persimmon tree and squeezed through the barbed wire fence to buy candy at the 7-Eleven across the street in Gum Springs.

We'd pass that same intersection driving to Route 1 and McDonalds. It was an original McDonalds with Golden Arches like giant buttresses. The night before a horse show mom would bring dinner from McDonalds to my sister and me. The smells of the greasy burgers and fries would waft through the big barn mingling with cedar shavings and saddle soap. We'd climb down from overturned buckets to sit and eat, country music blaring on the radio, our horses patiently waiting for us to finish braiding their manes.

One summer, since we didn't have the money to hire someone to haul our horses to a show, Kath and I rode them the four miles each way from Briary to Woodlawn Polo Club, starting south through the back roads of Gum Springs. We left early that Saturday morning, the air heavy and still, my body humming with excitement. Mom met us at Woodlawn, the station wagon filled with equipment and feed for the horses, folding chairs and a cooler with tuna sandwiches, pretzels and sodas. She stayed for a few hours to cheer us on, then left with a friend. Show days were marathons. When she came back in the late afternoon to pick up the car she consoled us for not winning any ribbons.

On the ride back to Briary, Kath and I slumped in our saddles, reins hanging slack as the horses trudged along. We were almost back to the barn as we wound through Gum Springs, which was pulsing with energy that hot summer night, filled with the smell of grilling meat and sound of laughter and radio music. A group of kids began following us, curious about the horses, I thought. But then someone yelled and threw a rock at us and others followed suit. I panicked, worried that they'd hurt Lady or Jeremy or make us fall off if the horses shied. We pushed our exhausted horses into a final burst of speed, galloping to safety.

That fall I started seventh grade at Stephen Foster, thrilled to be able to walk across the street to the barn after school. But in homeroom a black girl picked a fight and threw a desk at me. While Briary remained a safe and beloved place, it felt flanked by hostile territory. A year later we moved an hour east to Herndon, Virginia and the trouble continued. While waiting for the late bus a group of black kids asked repeatedly if I were a boy or a girl. I was skinny and flat-chested and had unwisely cut my hair into a short bob. Frustrated at my silence one of them kicked me, then fists started flying. I threw punches as I ran for the bus that finally arrived, then sat alone, angry and ashamed. The next day I was poked with a safety pin in the hallway and told by three girls to "come outside and talk about it" if I didn't like it. I started after them but new friends pulled me away.

Racial tension had been high in Herndon since white cops killed an unarmed black man in a local 7-Eleven store. What was happening to me was part of a bigger picture. I felt sick with fear and dread and sought help from the principal. He made the violence stop . . . at least for me. I was bright enough to see racial and class bias and didn't *want* to be prejudiced. Yet I had come to fear black people. My ancestors weren't descendants of slave owners. I didn't understand why I was a target for their rage.

When my father retired from the Army and took an aerospace job in Los Angeles, we sold the horses and moved to

Rancho Palos Verdes, an upscale white suburb. It took me a while to figure out what to do with myself without Lady and without the constant vigilance I'd learned. As I moved into adulthood I worked in fair housing and social justice in Los Angeles, hoping to build a better society, one where race didn't matter. But perhaps that was never the right dream.

A few years ago I read James Baldwin, who in *Notes of a Native Son* articulates why a colorblind society denies a black person the totality of his or her own history. If we no longer see color, "the Negro in America can only acquiesce in the obliteration of his own personality, the distortion and debasement of his own experience." Baldwin explains that the issues of race are "a fearful inheritance, for which untold multitudes, long ago, sold their birthright." Baldwin wrote essays to locate himself within that inheritance and to reclaim his birthright. Part of *my* fearful inheritance is white violence, the privileges it claims and the rage of its victims.

I recently learned that George Washington's former slaves founded Gum Springs when they were freed after his death in 1799. What I had dismissed as old shacks in my girlhood were rural freedmen's homes built sixty years before National Emancipation. Their leader, West Ford, is rumored to have been the son of a slave woman and an unidentified male of the Washington family.

As girls, my sister and I rode our horses from one former plantation to another, as privileged whites before us had done, through the streets of a proud, excluded community. And on that steamy summer evening in the Virginia twilight, as we galloped down the back streets of Gum Springs to escape those angry black children, we all had a small, bitter taste of our shared inheritance.

> It is not simply the relationship of oppressed to oppressor, of master to slave, nor is it motivated merely by hatred; it is also, literally and morally, a blood relationship, perhaps the most profound reality of the American experience, and we cannot begin to unlock it until we accept how very much it contains of the force and anguish and terror of love.
>
> – James Baldwin, *Many Thousands Gone*, 1951

When the Children Ask

MARILYN JOHNSTON

Dishman's Store sat on the Highway
that bisected our small town. To the north
was Richmond and to the South, the bridge
that crossed the Appomattox River,
like the Battle of the Crater separated
the Union and Confederate soldiers –
each end of the expanse large, entrenched.
Dishman's was our demilitarized zone,
where kids of any religion and color
could ride up on their bikes after school,
plunk their 5 pennies on the tall counter
and walk away with 5 pieces of something:
sugared jellies that stuck between our teeth,
or waxed lips that stained our faces,
or white candy cigarettes with bright red tips.
We'd hang around the side of the store
pretending we were inhaling and flicking
invisible ashes. Mama would yell

at my older brother and me if she heard
we'd been sighted at Dishman's,
scold us for riding our bikes near the highway.
But it was at Dishman's where we'd risk defiance,
where I still go in my imagination.
They say in the Appomattox, in those muddy waters,
that the spirit of a Confederate soldier still lurks
and will catch us if we cross the bridge unaware.
The child in my unsettled dreams is born into the place
I grew up – in the blood between North and South,
between Black and White water fountains
and Blacks in the back of the bus
and a rock that shattered our front door
with a note, *Dirty Jew*, rubber-banded around it.
One day I will take my granddaughters,
show them the empty lot where Dishman's
once stood. We'll walk the path to the highway,
then over the Appomattox Bridge
I last crossed late-August 1965,
hurrying to catch the bus for college,
suitcase banging against my leg.
In my dreams the children turn to me,
ask what we have learned from it all –
for them, their future?
And what do I tell them?

Saying Goodbye

JILL ELLIOTT

February 2013

I follow the nurse to my father's windowless hospital room and see him sitting on a chair.

"Mr. Elliott," she says in a perky voice, "I've got a surprise visitor for you."

He raises his head to her face, then looks to the doorway where I stand. When he smiles, I let out the breath I've been holding. I don't want him to think I've come to say goodbye, even though that's part of the reason I came.

"What on earth are you doing here?" he asks in a surprisingly strong voice.

I cross the room and bend over to hug him. I've never seen him wearing pajamas before, and don't remember him ever spending a day in bed. His arms clutch tight around me. I'm relieved he's sitting in a chair, not lying in a hospital bed, slumped and withered like so many of the other old men I passed on my way to his room.

"I'm here to get you out of here," I say. "I've come to take you home."

After he loosens his grip, I step back and sit on the edge of the bed, holding tight to his gaze. His blue eyes are red-rimmed and watery. His bones show through his thin skin. Bruises purple the backs of his hands. Rarely one to show emotions, he'd blow his nose into a crumpled cotton handkerchief when we parted at airports to disguise the wetness in his eyes. My eyes are likely red also, after too many hours in the dry air inside the three planes that brought me here from Portland, Oregon. I'm not complaining; I chose to leave the south of England when I was twenty-one, never considering my parents' end-of-life needs.

The hospital room is so hot and stuffy I can barely breathe. I remove my jacket and sweater and sit in my sleeveless shirt. Words spill from Dad's mouth like a waterfall cascading over rocks. He relates everything that's happened to him during his three-week confinement. I've heard most of it during phone calls with my brother and mother, who visit every evening for an hour.

"Your mother doesn't want me home." His voice quavers and his eyes pool. "She's having too much fun going out with her friends while I'm stuck in here."

It saddens me to see my father so vulnerable. The strong man who carried me when I tired of walking, towed cars out of mud with his Land Rover, dug my garden over, mixed and poured concrete, and built walls, has weakened into a frustrated man who can do little for himself.

Dad's biggest fear is that he'll die in a nursing home. He moved our family into his mother's home for the few weeks before she died, to take care of her. Mother has announced to anyone within earshot that she's no Florence Nightingale, and this isn't helping Dad's chances of dying in his own home. They'll need help, and now that I'm here I can arrange as much assistance as he will accept.

March 2013
My father and I sit by the window in what used to be the guest-room. This is not the house where I grew up, but it's in the same seaside town. The room is littered with his walker, shelves filled with Ensure, a basket of pill packets, and a hazardous waste container. The caregiver has changed his catheter, washed him, and dressed him in a clean pair of pajamas. All I have to do is be with him. One of mother's friends has taken her out shopping.

We look directly at one another across the table cluttered with prescriptions, mail, newspapers, and Soduko puzzles. Silence stretches between us. Is this the time I'm supposed to ask him which hymns he'd like sung at his funeral? I've had no experience with dying, taken no classes, nor sat any exams on the subject. Dad probably won't live until his ninety-second birthday in October, and this will likely be the last time I'll see him. Gulls swoop and land on the front lawn grabbing our attention.

"Look at those seagulls," he says. "They're stomping so the worms will think it's raining and they'll come out of the ground."

In the movies at life's end, there are poignant conversations, the sharing of secrets, and forgiveness. My father and I have never exchanged the words "I love you", and we don't break that tradition.

"Almost eleven," he says, glancing at the clock on the bookcase.

That's my cue to make instant black coffee. Dad's a creature of habit. He likes coffee and two digestive biscuits served promptly for his elevenses. I can do this simple thing for him.

June 2013

I watch cars pass from the window in what was my father's sickroom and compulsively check the time on my watch. Deep inside my body is a tightly coiled spring, ready to unravel at the slightest touch. Mother is in the bedroom selecting jewelry to go with her black suit and white blouse.

Earlier this foggy morning I walked along the seafront where seagulls shrieked, past the cricket field where Dad captained the cricket team before I was born, past the two houses where he grew up, and then returned to the house where he died. Instead of sitting in the chair where he last inhaled, I pace the room in my stockinged feet.

Head bent, the funeral director walks slowly along the road, in front of the black Mercedes. Mother comes into the room to ask if her slip shows. A black limousine parks behind the hearse and two men wearing black suits get out of the car and follow the funeral director up the driveway. Dad would appreciate that his last journey will be in such a prestigious and well-polished car. He took pride in his vehicles and washed them every Sunday while his legs still held his weight.

Heavy mist surrounds our small funeral procession as it makes its way across the Cuckmere River, past Friston Forest, and over the white cliffs where sheep graze. Dad watched lambs when he was driven home in an ambulance four months ago. Did he know it would be the last spring he'd see? This drive was his favorite, and mine.

The funeral goes as funerals do. I stand too early to read the poem I've chosen. I place my hands firmly on the podium so no one will notice them shake. I speak slowly and clearly and don't trip over my heels when I return to the pew. I hear Dad's voice in my head telling me I did the best I could.

April 2017

Had I known my father only had three months more to live, I could have put my life on hold and stayed with him. I would have found a taxi service that accommodated wheelchairs and taken him to the seaside. We'd have watched the seagulls and waves while eating ice creams with chocolate flakes. We'd have driven across the Cuckmere River, past Friston Forest, and along the white cliffs. We'd have stopped for a curry, or coffee cake, maybe both. We might have shared the stories that aren't written here.

The Verb Forms of Aging

LOIS RUSKAI MELINA

TENSE

Past: *I was born in 1952.*

Present: *I am 64 years old.*

Future: *The years after this will be different from anything I've known. They will not center on paid work, raising children, building a resume. How will I introduce myself?*

VOICE

Active: In the active voice, the subject is doing or becoming something: *I wonder how to find meaning in this new stage of my life; how to use my body, my talents, my voice. I notice how seldom people I meet ask me what I "do." I think they assume whatever I "do" is not interesting.*

Passive: In the passive voice, action is done to the subject, but the doer of the action is not identified: *I am asked more often if I need help carrying my groceries to the car.*

Colloquial use of the passive voice, using forms of "get" rather than forms of "be," allows us to feel the verb as an action rather than as a state: *I got blindsided by age because I was so involved in my life.*

The use of "become" shades the meaning further, showing it as the result of a development: *I became marginalized, unseen.* When the progressive form of "be," "get," and "become" are joined with a past participle, it indicates that the action goes on continuously: *I am getting ignored.*

MOOD

Indicative: The indicative mood states a fact, a close relation to reality. The subject experiences the action as an actual reality in daily life, one that must be reckoned with: *I grieve the loss of muscle tone, that my grandchildren live so far away, that I didn't prepare for retirement more thoughtfully, that I went after a more predictable career rather than doing what I really wanted – developing myself as a writer. The truth is, I didn't know if I was good enough to be the kind of writer I wanted to be. I ran away from my longing, back to the comfort of a position and a salary, back to what I knew I could do well.*

Subjunctive: Expresses a wish or desire that is outside reality or has little hope of being realized: *Sometimes I think that if I could do it over again, I would spend those years writing. But then I remember: I would not be the person I am, the writer I am. If I'd done it differently, I would not have the pain I have or the lessons I've learned. But I would have had other pains, other lessons. I wonder if I would have been a better writer, or if I'm a better writer for the path I took.*

Imperative: A command, admonition, warning: *Don't tell me how lucky I am that I have all this time now to write. Listen to what I'm telling you.*

NUMBER AND PERSON

First Person Singular: *Some days I struggle to write, and to believe in myself as a writer, and to believe that what I write has meaning for anyone but me.*

First Person Plural: *We went to a reading recently by a writer we admire.*

Third Person Singular. *A few days later, he revealed that he has a brain tumor. The prognosis is not good. He is my age. He's well known, successful, but he has more to say. He just wrote a story about what it's like when the unthinkable happens.*

Second Person Singular and Plural: *You never know.*

Third Person Plural: *They make new discoveries all the time.*

ASPECT

The character of the action is called the "aspect."

Terminate: The act is a finished whole, an actual truth; it is completed: *One day I decided to learn to row. I didn't consider what I would do with this new skill; I impulsively signed up for the course, paid in full, showed up ready to row. No one asked me what I did outside of the boat. When we hoisted the shell onto our shoulders to carry it from the boathouse to the water, no one asked me if I needed help. When I finished the class, I joined the rowing club.*

Progressive: Shows the act as habitual or ongoing and communicates more feeling: *I am rowing regularly now, getting up at 4 a.m. to be on the water by 5:00, even when it's dark or raining. I am feeling accepted, even though I am older than most of my teammates. I am even thinking about racing. My day consists of rowing, then writing (and sometimes napping).*

INFINITE FORMS

The participle is an adjective with the force of a verb: *The river is healing. The passion I feel for something new is rejuvenating me.* The participle is often passive: *Unconscious material is being brought to the surface when my body is moving in sync with the boat. Creative energy is being released.*

Originally, the infinitive was a noun, and it is now used as the subject or object of the verb: *To feel powerful – physically and mentally – is to feel more fully alive. To create is a way to find meaning at any age.*

TENSE FORMATION

Originally, there was no future tense in the English language. There was only the present and the past. The future was expressed in terms of the present or the past: *People who say that in retirement you just do more of what you did before rather than taking up the hobby you never got around to or fulfilling an unmet longing are not necessarily right. Maybe you discover what you were meant to do all along.*

What we call future tense always contains part of the present or part of the past: *I write stories so that my children and grandchildren and even strangers know me, even after I am gone, so that they know that I lived and what I longed for. I write so that I will not disappear.*

REFERENCE

The descriptions of verb forms are taken from *English Grammar* by George O. Curme (New York: Barnes & Noble, 1947).

My Most Vital Heart

MARE HAKE

I had spent the day crying, displaying what my father would have called "weakness." Growing up in suburban New Jersey I lost my father when I was sixteen, but by that time I hadn't lived with him for almost two years. His alcoholism began before I was born and grew every year alongside me until, by the time I was fourteen, he was hospitalized and I was beginning a long pilgrimage between other homes. I don't have very many memories of him, certainly none with adult perspective, but I do remember a few things. I know he fought in World War II, he was a decorated pilot over the European theater. I know he drank far too much rye whiskey, had scars he'd talk about only when drunk, and one day he explained to me how a man could snap his neck in a tree if a breeze caught his parachute and forced his death – he could be surprised just at the moment he might've thought he'd live through the searing metal wreckage. The unfairness of those seconds haunted him, he said, as I learned to serve him his coffee after dinner. All women should learn to serve, he said, and I believed him. Ask to serve, and approach from the same side. First the coffee, then the devil-tinted whiskey on the rocks. First the war, then the dead white scars.

When he died a few years later as a man in his mid-sixties, he'd lost his sense of time. He no longer knew what decade it was, or if we were at war, or if he had a daughter with my name. I wasn't as stunned then, as I should have been, to be forgotten. As a teenager I was accustomed to being overlooked and as his child, I knew once the whiskey kicked in, so did the war. His internal life was centered before my birth. But some said his forgetting was a final release, a gift of peace and absolution. It was nothing of the sort. Not knowing the war was over, he was always fighting it, trapped in a spiral web of all points leading to that crash like a gnat to the spider's mouth. Which crash? That crash. Breaking his own neck in a tree, or was it his co-pilot's neck? Did he feel that snap, or only hear it and in hearing it, relive the sound, the vision, of his friend's death every day he remained alive? Neither man who went into that tree came out the same. Earning the holes in his leg, again and again, my father's flesh as open and weeping as the thundering sky. Losing his friends, his plane, his safety, and some of his soul, flowing down the trousered leg into the French countryside to cover the old roots in steaming lines, a flowering red carnage. He was always hurt, never healed, never a man living in suburbia and raising his children. Without enough time to recover, he bled to death in his mind, over and over and over, in his clean hospital bed above the sloping gentle lawn and chilled autumn leaves, until his body finally released him.

So, women cry. Women are weak. I know he said that, and believed it, and if he'd lived, he likely wouldn't have voted for Hillary, unless in secret. And yet he wasn't a prejudiced man –

insides, he said, *are the same.* Only much later did it occur to me that he may have been speaking from memory. How many did he see die, I wonder, shot in the stomach with rapid fire ammunition until their intestines fell out and forward, or ripped in the chest with ignited-hot shrapnel until the blood-ied saliva bubbled out from the lead-pierced lungs in the tiny holes of complete devastation? How many insides did he see on the outside? Breath and blood and mucus and brain, and what would he have done with a president who never served, who actively avoided service, who said he was smarter than the generals into that national microphone on the big, shiny stage?

I'll never know for sure, but I wept for us that election night. I wept for the child I was, watching my father die over and over again, to save America from fascism. From ignorant, racist fools. To protect the innocent from the violent oppressor. To be brave. To do all of those things in radio silence . . . for in my life, I never saw him in uniform. Like the combat pilot he was, he never advertised his position, he never let the shape of his heroism be a target for the anti-aircraft guns. He didn't wear his medals or march on Veteran's day because he didn't have to. He knew what he'd done and what it cost him to do it.

It's from his strength that I move forward, hauling my torn parachute behind me, my big armload of rope and broken material hard to grasp and I'm limping from my branch-torn muscles. A shredded tendon of loss that was twisted is now straight and points the way, while the blood seeping across my shirt has formed a second skin, cold and damp and cam-ouflaged across the top of my most vital heart. My eyes have dried and I no longer weep behind a closed door, but walk the same path once marked in the woods of France, the way of personal resistance against violence and terror, a courage marked by the potholes and mud and granite-hard voices of all who have come this way before and refused to be lost, even in the darkest night.

Star Stuff

KALI LIGHTFOOT

The apples will not care
that I didn't walk this morning
or never learned a second language
or read Proust
or was not a better supervisor.

Knowing that atoms of my body come from stars
that died five billion years ago
and will be available
five billion years from now in some other body
or star
or drop of water
or apple lying in the orchard path
is oddly comforting.

Red and purple sunsets from the bluff above the pond
or Katahdin on a full moon night
or "Silent Night" sung by candlelight

or the smiles of my grandsons
will be of no consequence to a drop of water.

I will be as dust drifting
on a solar wind,
beyond atmosphere
and planet, untroubled and unconscious.
This much-worried, much-loved life,
atoms strewn across a galaxy of galaxies.

Prelude to Catherine Creek

SETH MICHAEL WHITE

September 3, 2015 – Union County, Oregon
Three days after my mother passed, I dreamt death was a country just around the corner, an expanse of sagebrush and juniper.

Today, nearly one year later, I'm standing on the bank of Catherine Creek watching a colossal salmon hold her place in the current. She has come here to spawn, but it's late season and most spawning is over. In June the rivers were already a trickle, and by July many of the feeder streams had run dry.

So I'm a little surprised (and a lot delighted) to meet the salmon here. Her dorsal fin is spotted white and waving like a surrender flag. Blotchy patches of fungus on her side prove her thousands-of-miles, years-long journey from this river to the ocean and back.

Salmon are often the centerpiece metaphor in the story of redemption and return, and rightly so. But I look around to notice other animals join in the throng: water ouzel; king-fisher; the delicate strips of a paper wasp nest; and, for reasons that are a deep mystery to me, a squirrel performing frenzied acrobatics on a cottonwood branch.

In knee-high rubber boots, I walk along the shore with forceps, scalpel, and collection vials, jotting notes in my field book. I am tracing the sources of food that will feed the salmon's progeny. The leaves of black hawthorn sink to the streambed and are eaten by a cranefly larva; cranefly becomes a succulent treat for a young fish. Waving green algae on the cobbles is scraped off by a casemaker caddisfly; caddisfly emerges from her stone shelter and becomes a tasty morsel. A mayfly escapes the river as a winged adult and becomes trapped in the web of a long-jawed spider. Spider ponders the river at dusk and is caught unawares by the bat.

I turn one last time to the salmon in the river. She will be gone in a matter of days. My mother's doctor had found what she thought was breast cancer, but after a barrage of tests the diagnosis morphed into stage IV lung cancer. Within a few short months, my mother crossed into that dream-country of sagebrush and juniper.

October 31, 2016 – Arlene Schnitzer Concert Hall, Portland
I'm in the house of the dead, braced in my seat, clenching the armrests. Below me on the stage, musicians in formal black attire sway with their instruments. This is Leoš Janáček's Prelude to *From the House of the Dead*, and the Oregon Symphony is delivering the piece to me, and a few hundred other fellow souls, spectacularly. Our collective pleasure ricochets off the ornate Renaissance contours of the Hall.

But I'm caught off guard. I thought tonight's program would be cutesy ghouls and ghosties, more treat than trick. Instead my heart thumps with the thunderous drum behind the grand sweeping strings, which repeat like crashing breakers on a rocky shore. Here come the creepy violins (the precursor to every modern horror flick) and their quick, high-pitched streams of dissonant notes. The melody is winning enough to beckon me – I follow willingly – yet discordant enough to lead me down a dark alley. Suddenly, I'm disconnected and alone, failing to recognize the landmarks.

From the program notes, I learn this was Janáček's take on Fyodor Dostoyevsky's autobiographical novel. Under tyrannical rule, Dostoyevsky spent four years' hard labor in a Siberian prison camp for his part in a literary discussion group. Life in the camp was more than brutal. Among the prisoners, he describes "corruption and terrible perversity. Backbiting and scandal-mongering."

"This was Hell," Dostoyevsky writes, "the nethermost pit and the outer darkness."

Janáček must have a found a morbid kinship with Dostoyevsky. The darkness of the Prelude is said to have originated from an incident Janáček witnessed during the General Strike in England: "Among the workers, things are boiling," he wrote. "Today they shot a driver in the street, for no reason at all."

And yet.

And yet, how does Janáček describe the underlying theme of *House*? The barbaric nature of humanity? The despotism of the ruling class? The injustice of everything? Instead, written on the score in Janáček's own handwriting: "In every being a spark of God."

Here, Janáček extends an olive branch to *Homo sapiens*, a testament to a faith in humanity's benevolence, even under the cruelest circumstances.

In every being a spark of God.

The playful trill of bright horns breaks the symphony's tension. But the reprise is short lived. Three defiant beats of the drum conclude the Prelude, hinting at the darker movements to come.

November 9, 2016 – Lloyd District, Portland

I don't need to understand the evolution of stars to do my work, but the notion that my methods depend on the first three seconds after the big bang is somehow enthralling.

Today, nearly two years after my mother's death, I'm in the laboratory preparing the Catherine Creek samples. I portion the samples into vials that I will ship to another lab in Flagstaff. Miniscule quantities of detritus, algae, moss, leaves, insects, and fish tissue will be analyzed with a mass spectrometer for their elemental compositions, providing clues on how nutrients and energy move through the river food web.

Due to a quirk in stellar nucleosynthesis, some elements like carbon and nitrogen exist in twin forms – stable isotopes – whose ratios change at predictable rates with biological reactions. My methods piggyback on this mystery, and verify Walt Whitman's claim that "a leaf of grass is no less than the journey-work of the stars."

I would like to talk to my mother about all this. I imagine we are having coffee. Bright morning sun gleams through the kitchen window. She cups the ceramic mug in her particular way. The coffee smells good: a rich earthiness, but with an undercurrent of sage and juniper.

We talk about the election for a while in the manner people we know talk about the election. You can wake up one morning and feel completely out of touch with your fellow Americans, people you once called neighbors. She shakes her head. I stare through the motes of dust. Maybe there is no way to understand. Discerning this, the poet William Stafford cautions us to vigilance: "The darkness around us is deep."

Our talk shifts to the salmon, the one on Catherine Creek who came back. She was a statistical outlier defying the odds of an anomalous drought. Yet a changing climate means drought will become more common in the years ahead. The survival of the salmon and her young will depend, more than ever, on robust or tenuous connections: the mayfly, the caddisfly, the algae and the long-jawed spider. The black bear scavenging the spawned-out carcass, trailing nitrogen back into the forest. The tribal fisherman perched on the rough-hewn wooden planks of a fishing platform. The dam operator with hands ready on the spillway controls.

If all goes right, each behemoth fish will return to Catherine Creek carrying hints of already-extinct stars from the early universe: carbon isotopes, nitrogen isotopes, also faith. Not knowing what else to do, I follow the sparks.

Drowning in Sorrow:
"I Have No Choice but to Keep Looking"

LEAH STENSON

The article on the front page of the *New York Times* told the story of a woman who, five years after the tsunami and nuclear disaster, prepares an obento, a traditional Japanese lunch box, for her daughter and throws it into the sea off the coast of northeastern Japan. She believes her daughter is there in some form, somewhere, tossed by the waves. It consoles her to remember her deceased daughter in this way. The woman's husband has taken up scuba diving in the hope of finding their daughter's remains.

I found myself drawn to the article because I have a deep connection to Japan: I lived there for sixteen years and I've visited the nuclear exclusion zone in Fukushima where I witnessed firsthand the aftermath of the tsunami and met nuclear refugees displaced from their homes. To be honest, I was also drawn in by the darkness and immediacy of the image of the husband's head in face mask and snorkel protruding above the surface of the dark water. Of course I was saddened to read about the personal tragedy of these victims of the tsunami, but I was disturbed by aspects of the article that were sensationalistic. The author discussed in detail the various stages of decomposition of corpses found underwater and even went so far as to speculate whether the daughter's bones might still be shrouded in the garments she was wearing when she drowned. Surely, more pressing and less gratuitously gruesome stories deserve our attention.

The devastation following the earthquake and tsunami was indeed catastrophic, but the event was nevertheless a 'singularity,' whereas the nuclear disaster in Fukushima remains dire and ongoing: the clean-up is plagued by the non-stop flow of contaminated groundwater, the ever-burning nuclear cores, lack of viable solutions for dealing with the environmental consequences, and the ongoing plight of thousands of nuclear refugees who remain homeless. In the face of these daunting problems, it is easy to give in to depression and despair. However, unlike the earthquake and tsunami—a *casus fortuitous* or *Force majeure* beyond our control—the antecedents to nuclear disasters lie within the scope of human responsibility and decision making. We need the unvarnished facts so we can learn from our mistakes. We also need hope and the courage to take correct action in the future.

As I watched the nuclear disaster unfold in Fukushima, I felt powerless along with the rest of the world but resisted giving in to hopelessness. I wanted to do something—anything— that might make a difference. I determined to use my voice as a poet to draw attention to the dangers of nuclear power, so two years after the meltdowns I published an anthology of poems by Japanese poets in an effort to help those impacted by the disaster speak to the world beyond the borders of Japan.

The simple act of publishing the book empowered me and affirmed my belief that we are capable of changing our world one person at a time, one small action at a time.

I want to hear more stories that inspire, stories that give people hope and the courage to take action, despite seemingly overwhelming challenges. On a recent trip to Japan, I met many people who were engaged in the struggle to raise awareness of the dangers of uranium-based nuclear power: a school teacher who had the courage to fight for many years against the siting of the nuclear power plant in Fukushima, despite being ostracized by his community; a nuclear refugee who conveyed through poetry and song the pain of being forced from his ancestral home; a publisher whose decades-long mission has been to warn his countrymen of nuclear accidents and the danger inherent in nuclear power. I would prefer to read articles about such everyday heroes.

Despite the catastrophic human and economic tragedy of Fukushima, the Japanese government seems intent on restarting the country's fifty-plus reactors. As of May 2017, two reactors are now operational and twenty-four are in the process of being approved for restart. This seems incomprehensible because a majority of the Japanese are opposed to restarting the reactors. Even former Prime Minister Naoto Kan, in office at the time of the nuclear disaster, has come out as firmly opposed. Given the gravity of the situation, we need patience, persistence, courage and especially hope. Thus, rather than publishing articles that leave the reader feeling hopeless or depressed, I encourage the *Times* to publish human interest stories that inspire and motivate us. Many people are working hard in different arenas to improve the state of our world, not just in Fukushima, and we need to hear their stories. It is people like these who can inspire us, who can be our role models, our beacons of hope.

By featuring a sensationalistic story about individual suffering instead of information about the ongoing catastrophe and efforts to bring authentic remediation, the newspaper missed an opportunity to inspire its readers and give them hope in dark times. Many of us are drowning in a tidal wave of sorrow, assaulted daily by stories of war, killing, corruption and hate. Rather than flood us with feelings of despair, I hope the news media will strive more diligently to provide us with information that empowers and motivates, that helps us keep our heads above water as we chart a course to a more informed, safe and compassionate world.

REFERENCE

The New York Times, "I Have No Choice but to Keep Looking," August 2, 2016.

Cracks in my Armor

RACHAEL DUKE

At twenty-two-years old I flew from Worthington, Ohio to Portland, Oregon for an entry level health worker job in an abortion clinic. The Portland Feminist Women's Health Center was on SE Foster Road near the Pietro's Pizza where two decades later my husband would have to attend baseball coach meetings and where Russian and Mexican restaurants share the street with plumbing, lumber and gun stores. Back then SE Foster was even grittier and the clinic was in a pale gray building with bars over the windows. On clinic days a parade of anti-abortion protestors lined the streets praying and pushing baby carriages around. I knew them by name and they knew me. Eventually, they also opened a storefront underneath the clinic, their front door next to our door, and in the windows they featured gruesome pictures of enormous fetuses and full- term babies as botched abortions. It was a war.

Working at the clinic was certainly like being in a battle. A mail bomb was detonated outside in the streets, some of our doctors had to wear bullet proof vests because of death threats, and once the "antis" followed my friend, a student from Sri Lanka, as she evasively maneuvered her way home on a bike.

She also had to listen to their racist name calling. The list of slurs included the name "Sheela," known as the accomplice of Bhagwan Shree Rajneesh who had just tried to take over Antelope, Oregon and had recently poisoned customers at a Wendy's Hamburgers salad bar in The Dalles, Oregon.

We were careful about our safety inside and outside work. We all were required to leave contact information with the clinic if we were going to be anywhere besides work during business hours. In an age before cell phones, clinic staff had to know how to get hold of me if the clinic received a package that was not immediately identifiable. More than once I answered the phone at home. I even received a call during a doctor appointment, and on the line was a co-worker asking me to confirm I had ordered something or other that had just arrived and was slightly unfamiliar. One afternoon a couple of us stopped and had a beer at a nearby bar on the way home. The clinic director yelled at us for an hour – did we understand the danger we put ourselves in?

My dreams were bloody and filled with exploding buildings. I made my roommates lock the door out of fear, something they had never done before and resented. I did not fully understand I had signed up to be a soldier. I just wanted to do what I believed was right.

The work was hard and intense, sometimes sad, and I carried it with me all the time. I could smell the sour almost tangy smell of fetal tissue mixed with the chemicals we used in the lab for hours after work; I can still smell it now, thirty years later, if I think hard enough. I would see the protestors out and about, maybe on the bus or on a city street somewhere, and would feel breathless and vulnerable. But I loved the moments of connection with our patients and I knew I was making a huge difference for the women that I helped to have a safe, affordable, and respectful abortion. Sometimes women who had been to the clinic would see me walking about the city and I could see them trying to place how they knew me. For every person who crossed the street to avoid making contact, another person would come up and take my hands and thank me for being there. It was the first time I realized how we can all be a bridge to another person; that we can help someone get from one place to the next place they need to be and how powerful that is. I felt strong. I deeply cared about my co-workers. I was turning into an adult.

But when you fight in a war you don't have the luxury to consider the gray and nuanced, anything that is a distraction from the mission. In retrospect I know this was true at the clinic, and that it was a struggle for me, but I wasn't fully aware of this experience until I learned it later from watching my brother. At the beginning of the Gulf War my brother, a West Point graduate, was thoughtful and circumspect about our engagement with Iraq and Kuwait in the shadow of our dependency on oil. Until his friends were there fighting. Then that conversation was over. It was all about the people he knew there and how to support them. Similarly, at the clinic, there was not a lot of space to talk about how much grief we witnessed, the pain people held, the fear that washed over the rest of our lives, because we had to be very very careful to not approach any kind of sentiment that seemed as if it was not fully in support of abortion or the boundaries we set. No cracks in the armor for understandable reasons, but the armor is heavy to wear.

I never really learned how to wear it either. Armor keeps the wearer safe and this includes ideological armor. But for me to understand and process my experiences every day, I needed something much more permeable, open to the environment around me. Something less safe and lighter, porous, but ultimately more sustainable. This was not possible for me to do. When I left the clinic it was less about the work and more about the weight that followed me around. When I started a new job at a bookstore I thought, *well thank god I don't have to do that anymore.* I was relieved but disoriented and the night after my last day, in Big Lebowski style, I got drunk on White Russians at a dive bar near the house where I lived. When I went to sleep that night the world was spinning around my bed.

Over time, even as I found new work that mattered, I learned that there is also a cost to the heart when you give up your place and the surety of purpose while an important battle goes on without you. I did think that it would get better, that the curve was in the right direction despite ongoing setbacks in violence against doctors and clinics, and more recently in distressing anti-choice legislation around the country. But I see now that wars don't really end. Sometimes those on the losing side just wait for a small shift to open up the possibility of a changed outcome. This means we are essentially always in combat when it comes to human rights, including the right for a woman to control her own body. The world still spinning along a battered and narrow orbit.

I know, even though it was hard and sad, that I was blessed to work at that clinic. I also am grateful for the cracks, in whatever armor I wear, that don't let me get too focused or comfortable with a single mission or purpose. Even when I desperately know something to be true there is still a little room for something else – grief, tolerance, compassion, hope. In the end, this is the imperfect armor I choose to wear in a world where we have to keep fighting.

III

FINDING OUR WAY FORWARD

My Mother Sends me a New Year's Message

SUZY HARRIS

Each dawn, the sky stretches its
silver dome like a canvas
for the bare branches
to write the day's story,
if we only knew how to read it.

The truth is, we want to create
our own story, attach one word
to another, syllable by syllable,
sentence by sentence.

And this is the miracle – each dawn,
we get to start the story over again,
word by word. Who says we can't
rewrite the script? Who says fear
always has to win?

Be the bare branch.
Be the silvery sky.

Come Shining: November 9, 2016
DIANE JOSEFOWICZ

The night after the election, I slipped out to join perhaps a hundred others gathered to remember the poet C. D. Wright. I'd met her only once, and, to the extent that I knew her at all, it was through her work. But I knew enough to understand that her loss – sudden, inexplicable – was the sort that went beyond the individual and her immediate circle to raise its hand against a whole community.

Maybe this sounds familiar.

Before leaving I'd made a salad for my daughter and a pot of mac-and-cheese. I wasn't running for mother of the year. The night was warm, unseasonable.

Wright's friends had planned the tribute, scheduled it for the day after the general election. Walking out that evening, I imagined they felt the date was safe, that grief would not be compounded by events. The result was, to say the least, equivocal, which the poet would have appreciated. This is my report: what she might have called an *elegiac procedure*.

The first words were hers. From high up her voice came down, a recording of the poet working herself into a moment, working a moment into a poem. It was a task I recognized: to couple one's words to their independent music which, like all independent things, demanded exact expression.

> *a bed is left open to a mirror*
> *a mirror gazes long and hard at a bed*

Through these cadences, reports of what she heard and over-heard, her presence emerged – her clarity, her anger, her reticence. Daughter of a lawyer and a law clerk, she knew about mistakes, about pulled punches and the risks of being merely polite. She knew more about courage. She knew most about power, the force of her inward voice gathering as she turned it out, stretching and loosening against silence. Her gift was to hear this music and to make others hear it, too.

> *"Didn't I hear you tell them you were born*
> *on a train"*

She had presided over the poets of the English department, a loose-jointed, long-limbed presence. When she died, she was sixty-seven. Many people in the room were her age, or older. Night came on. The wind picked at the floating trees, troubling the leaves.

One after the other, her friends took positions at the podium. Rivals had mellowed into comrades-in-arms, sorehearted wooers paid their respects by proclaiming, loyally, that their hearts were still sore. Would always be. She inspired devotion. Does the arc of history bend – truly, loyally, devotedly – toward justice? Through what medium must history be projected in order to create this happy refraction?

Come shining.

The question was alive that night. Our gathering – our devotion – animated the question.

The first words her friend ever heard her say:

You ain't heard of Watergate?

The weighted line falls down through dark water, falls until the line gives or bottoms out. A feeling filled the room and billowed outward, like a sail. I sat as still as I could, adding my breath to it. If the future is to be worth having, words must be found and made to fit, dovetailed to emergent music.

A smell on my hands, herbal, familiar – the lemon I'd sliced before leaving. A scent I could not place until I could.

night of coon scat and vandalized headstones
night of deep kisses and catamenia

Her friends named places they'd known her: Providence, Santiago, her student pad at Fayetteville. Every grief will have its own geography.

I was the poet of short-tailed cats and yellow
line paint.
Of satellite dishes and Peterbilt trucks.
The poet of yard eggs and
sharpening shops,
jobs at the weapons plant and the Maybelline
factory on the penitentiary road.

In Fayetteville, the heartsore eulogist said, the newlyweds Bill and Hillary Clinton had occasionally visited, young and idealistic and expecting to live distinguished lives. He remembered Bill from those days, "his fierce intelligence only partly masked" by his hick persona. "All of it seemed sanctified."

Except for Bill's wife, whom the writer admired less. Like her husband, she, too, always appeared slightly masked, her eyes lost behind smudged lenses. "Poor Hillary," he said, looking up from his notes as if to find and rebuke the American electorate hiding somewhere in the rafters.

Outside, a hissing leaf-shift, but *shh*, it's only the wind.

He'd smudged the lenses himself, of course – smudged them with whatever he needed her to be that she wasn't. Say, electable. I'm certain she knew she was up against the old problem having no value on the marketplace of cis white male desire. They didn't want her, never did. Their wives voted with their interest, which has always been to keep the peace at home. She was not running for mother of the year.

You didn't know my weariness, error, incapacity

What she couldn't say to those voters: Your loyalty will not save you. Domesticity will not save you. Not mastery of cooking or the rules of football. Not devotion to dishtowels, to spotless toilet bowls.

I'd done it, too: looked back, gone back. Foundered on the discovery of just how much difference my family was prepared to tolerate. It wasn't much. Wright went back to her home places too, chronicling lives of the women who lived there, in the prisons, up the penitentiary road.

The poet knew who she was and what she was up against, the forces that wanted her to be something else. She spoke for those on the lost roads, the places unrepresented, neither spoken of nor spoken for; where language avails nothing as a matter of conscious and intentional policy. Her words revealed the dark seams of injustice marking those dumbstruck roads.

These images twist like sheets on a hot Fayetteville night circa 1970, or like the flyblown paper helices twisting in my grandmother's kitchen on a Providence night of the same temperature and vintage. I want to bring those worlds together: a hot house, a sticky surface, a twisting piece of paper, a smudged lens,

a surface tension of the sort we call meaning.

The morning after the election, I snapped a photograph of a

shop window that had been spray-painted: RIP, USA. 1776-
2016. I passed young women weeping in the street. Overnight,

ordinary life had become an extreme sport.

The task was to see what was in front of me, to shine a light
across a factual surface, to illuminate the grit and smear. The
bits of self that are not to be discarded, even when our loved
ones ask us to, threatening to discard us. Inclusivity means
anything can happen, including what was unthinkable before.
A sonnet might have thirteen lines or sixteen. Your personal
future might include a thrown punch. Or a run for office. What
I am trying to say: we are now living in a C. D. Wright poem.
Our task is the one she knew inside out, what she showed us
with her diction, her syntax, her lived example:

to walk down the road without fear.

REFERENCE
The italicized texts are taken from C. D. Wright, "Our Dust," *String Light*
(University of Georgia Press, 1991); and from eulogies transcribed by the
author at Wright's memorial on November 9, 2016, in Providence, RI.

A Stick Chart for the Time of Trump

EDWARD WOLF

Palm-rib staves tied with twine form a lattice roughly two feet on a side. Eleven staves cross the lattice on the diagonal. Four more, of varying lengths, lace through the grid and the diagonals in the top right corner. Twenty-three polished cowrie shells are lashed to the lattice, singly and in clusters like constellations.

This curious object, a Polynesian stick chart, hangs on the wall behind my writing desk. I contemplate its spare beauty. I ponder its meaning.

Agitated by the news-cycle circus of early 2017, I take solace in the stick chart's delicate geometry. Recently I've begun to peel back layers of its story: layers of tradition and memory embedded in the object itself. Layers of battle and bravery that shaped the man who brought it to Oregon after World War II. Layers that recall a dark time, and the journey that led that man out of the darkness.

Polynesian stick charts, anthropologists tell us, model the flux of the sea. The ribs depict ocean swells as they reflect and refract among coral atolls in the South Pacific. The cowries represent islands. Each stick chart displays wave patterns reliable enough to guide navigation among distinct island groups.

The master navigators who made stick charts were renowned for their ability to steer seafaring canoes while lying in the bottom of the boat. By sensing the size and spacing of swells encountered en route, a traditional Polynesian mariner could chart a flawless passage across hundreds of miles of open water.

On the Sunday before Thanksgiving in 1943, a young U.S. Navy coxswain stood at the helm of an amphibious Higgins boat riding swells off Betio Island, 2,400 miles southwest of Hawaii. A coral-fringed island like those depicted by stick-chart cowries, Betio makes up the southwestern extremity of the Tarawa atoll, modern capital of the nation of Kiribati.

It was not a place any sailor would have chosen to spend that day. The U.S. Fifth Fleet had targeted the heavily defended island, site of a Japanese airfield, for invasion. The Battle of Tarawa was a high-stakes gamble intended to break the stalemate that prevailed between Allied forces and Japan two years after Pearl Harbor. Dozens of warships and tens of thousands of men deployed for the campaign. Higgins boats would deliver regiments from the 2nd Marine Division to Betio's reef for the shore assault.

The invasion began before sunrise on Saturday, November twentieth. Through Sunday, the battle with Betio's defenders raged. Higgins boats held positions off the reef, attempting to support Marines as they crossed the beach despite sustained fire from onshore batteries. One boat managed a daring rescue, retrieving thirteen wounded Marines imperiled on the reef by a rising tide. The skipper kept his head and pulled his craft and the injured Marines back to safe waters under incendiary fire, while his crew stamped out bullets that flamed on deck.

Betio fell and the Battle of Tarawa ended in victory for the Allied forces, though heavy casualties and news photos showing scorched-earth devastation shocked the American public. The rescue of the thirteen Marines on Betio's reef, just a few moments out of the seventy-six hour engagement, earned a mention in the seventh volume of Samuel Eliot Morison's *History of the United States Naval Operations in World War II.* Describing the rescue, Morison expressed admiration for "the cool, impeccable seamanship of this boat's unidentified coxswain."

The coxswain was an Oregonian named Ralph Austin Grenfell, Jr. He survived the three-day battle and the twenty-one months of war that followed the assault on Betio, and returned to his family home in Eugene. A year after V-J Day he married his wartime sweetheart, a pretty young nurse-in-training named Betsy Nygaard, and moved to Reedsport to start a career as a state wildlife biologist. Among the few mementos he carried from his tour in the Pacific was the Polynesian stick chart.

Ralph and Betsy were my wife's godparents. I never knew Ralph, who passed away before Karen and I married. The stick chart occupied a place of honor on the wall of Betsy's small home in the years after his death, but she never spoke of it. Though Betsy loved nothing more than talk of Ralph and the life they had shared, I don't recall ever hearing her mention the seamanship that had earned him a page in history.

Here's the thing: the Polynesian navigators who made stick charts left them ashore. Each chart was one man's personal mind-map of the sea. A navigator fitted palm ribs and cowries into the pattern needed to provision his memory before an up-coming voyage. I like to imagine that a mariner so provisioned could face with confidence the unplanned events – the squalls, the mishaps, the sudden turns of fortune – that write the story of any journey.

Betsy's stories of Ralph conjured a man whose playful sense of humor hid a reflective turn of mind. Had he returned to Oregon with memories enough for a dozen stick charts of his own? Did the palm-rib artifact mounted on their wall sig-nify his internal map to safety through the savage battles in the Pacific?

Like a well-crafted story, a stick chart reveals a person deeply engaged with the world. The evidence it shares is hope-ful – that the world can be known, that a daunting journey may be navigated. Whether a traveler is faced with the fog of war, a chaotic political moment, or an expanse of restless seas, stories and stick charts alike argue for faith in the future.

A man. A boat. A battle. Palm ribs. Cowries. Twine. A story and an artifact, each tells its tale of "cool, impeccable seaman-ship" in the waters of the South Pacific. The stories we need to write, read, and share are like the stick chart that now hangs beside my desk, its handcrafted artistry a reminder: this un-ruly world is full of patterns that can guide us safely home.

Conditions of Happiness

ANNIE LIGHTHART

Take a bed in a quiet room and wake
without pain –

a kingdom is not necessary.
Just as one bird proves flight is possible,

a crumb of bread
establishes sun and wheat,

establishes heat, attests to the presence
of a loaf and hand.

When you do not measure time,
each day is a little year,

the whole expanse in miniature,
every season

an occasion for peace.
You have what you need

is what the birds sing all morning,
and the small boat on the river

tells us again –
If there is no wind, then row.

Yes (and No)

SUZY HARRIS

In this new year, the sun
cracks through the cold,
illuminates the dust motes,
makes them dance in the shafts of light.

Yes to this light.
Yes to the cleansing, piercing cold.
Yes to the breath that creates its own crystalline form.
Yes to the muddy paths through the bare trees,
and yes to the persistent hummingbirds.

Always the new year brings a feeling like
the first day of school or
unfolding a tablecloth.

Now, fear is driven to the smallest place –
a shoebox stashed in the attic

or a tin buried in the compost pile –
still there, yes, but not in charge.

No, today the clear bright sunlight
takes us by the hand,
points the way forward.

The Writer's Faith

DAVID OATES

Not long ago I gave a reading at a Portland bookstore. The typical deal: eight listeners, one cat, one sale. They all seemed so engaged – the humans. I thought it went well.

It is hard to sell a book. Hard to place a poem or an essay. Yet getting work into the hands of readers is the mission and reward of writing. Not necessarily a million readers: I think we seek the *right* readers. I've come to believe in this quite strongly. Writing seems to be a faith without any doctrine, a faith found only in the practice of it. For what else could it mean, to write things down? Only that readers exist, out there somewhere, a shadowy *unknown* whose intelligence and good will we assume, and work in the spirit of, and try to be faithful to. Day in, day out. Early and late. Jotting notes. Hunching over the keyboard. Taking a walk to sort it all out. Quitting for the day, but always getting up tomorrow to continue.

I speak from experience, of a sort: I am a minor author. Have been for decades. Few, oh very few, know my name. It's hard to find my books. I can't make a living at it, not directly. Yet I am cheerful in this life. Why? Why?

Because I have this confidence, this faith. It gives me joy.

Once, I shrugged and sent a pretty-good poem to a ridiculously obscure place – the weekly poetry niche in our regional newspaper. Nothing could be more fleeting, a guaranteed one-day run, as far from my long-desired marquee in *Poetry* magazine as could be imagined. It ran, it disappeared, I forgot about it.

A few years later I was included in a reading organized by one of my longtime writing students: three poets in a Friends Church on the other side of town. And when I met Peggy, the third reader, she was practically kvelling. A middle-aged woman! And over *me*? "I cut out that poem about the trout. I stuck it on my writing desk, where I could see it every day. *That's* how I want to write."

Is this important? Not for agents or big-name publishers it isn't. Neither Farrar nor Straus nor Giroux has come knocking. But important? Perhaps. In some way much harder to define.

This is a sort of hearsay gospel, isn't it? The Writing Evangel: something good is happening somewhere. Most of the time we never hear it or see it. But we believe in it, or we ought to.

When I finally ran into Lewis Hyde's book *The Gift,* I felt, as many readers must, that something basic had been revealed, something I recognized immediately but had never heard voiced. That if we are bearers of a gift – even a small gift, like mine – then we must treat it as surplus, as abundance, as something to be shared.

The secret power of writing – the act of writing, the life of writing – is this baseline of generosity. Writing is an attempt to give of oneself. To take one's gift of language, feeling, and insight, and offer it to whosoever comes. As Adrienne Rich says (of poetry): writing "comes out of silence, seeking connection with unseen others." From this logic of giving, all good things are possible. The heart is kept clean. And joy is available, even in the forgotten corners where unremarked writers labor, and meet each other for beers once a week, and go to each other's little readings, and share in the small breakthroughs and oh-so-local moments of recognition.

The money life, commodification sales fame bankability, is based on the logic of scarcity. It must crowd someone else out, dominate the market. It cannot understand what I am talking about. The importance of a single reader? Too few pennies to measure.

Certainly a writer needs *some* readers. Mozart said he didn't "write for the drawer," and neither should we. Maybe just a few readers. . . or even that one true reader. That one who will be touched and changed. And whom the writer will probably never meet. Yet she's out there. He lives somewhere. This reader, these readers – they go on in the world, unnoticed (like me, like most of us), and something spreads out from them too, something invisible. Some wholeness, some healing, some seeing or taking up of courage. And I believe some of this force in the world, some of this heart and connectedness, comes from my words. *My words.*

That's all I need.

I have other examples but here's my favorite. Maybe someone reading this can help me with it, for I can't document the story. All I know is, I heard it from another believer, in a radio interview a few years ago. A writer, he spoke with authority. But I was on the freeway, had to teach all day and grade papers all evening, forgot to write down his name. . . . But here's the story, the good news that came to me anyway.

The Burmese democracy-activist and politician Aung San Suu Kyi, for the crime of winning 59% of the vote in 1990, was sentenced to fifteen years of house arrest under the government of the Generals. Her imprisoning house by the lake was full of bookshelves. She read all the Harry Potter books. She read detective novels. She read Victor Hugo and George Eliot.

And she read a little book by this American author I heard on the radio. Somehow it had ended up on a shelf in Burma. It was about nonviolent political heroes, Thoreau, Gandhi, Martin Luther King, and some lesser-knowns – people who had persevered under terrible privation and duress. It was a book that had sold, he said, "ten copies and then disappeared." A book that was part of his discouragement, his failure as a writer, he said. Later he become more successful and got to talk on interview shows. But he said that he liked to think about that little book, that failure. How one of its few copies – the rest all unsold, remaindered, cut up – how that one sole copy had come into the hands of Aung San Suu Kyi, to give her some little measure of strength and heart to continue on her path as one of the world's fighters against repression.

Sometimes, one reader is enough.

In the mindset of abundance, we give it away, to be measured by chance and by mystery – not by dollars. Our Portland poet the late William Stafford, though well known and even celebrated, never thought himself too grand to say "yes" to a high-school or middle-school English class. Or to a book club – eight readers and a cat. He was always willing, he would read simply and from the heart to a national audience or to a gathering of nobodies.

If a larger audience should offer to come to me, I will welcome it. As anyone would. Until then, I continue content. For ours is a secret economy. We thrive without being noticed. We connect and offer, give and receive. We are the lucky ones. We know what counts. And we give it away.

Adapted from a talk at Whidbey Island Writers Association, August 2013

REFERENCES

Adrienne Rich, "The Hermit's Scream," in *What is Found There: Notebooks on Poetry and Politics* (New York: Norton, 1993) p. 57.

Lewis Hyde, *The Gift: Creativity and the Artist in the Modern World* (New York: Vintage, 2007).

"We give it away" is derived from the Elizabeth Woody poem "Spider Woman's Coyote Bones," in her *Seven Hands, Seven Hearts* (Portland, Ore.: Eighth Mountain, 1994) pp. 89-91.

Reparations

PAULANN PETERSEN

Let the Sun-Woman still live
in her house named Sun-Wheel –
her no-sided, all-sided home,
a ray-roomed place of residence.

Let each of her arms reach
the curve of those rounded walls,
her fingers touching the bowed glass
of every bay window. Such windows
are numbered enough for her light
to find its way out and into
the all of this world.

Her rays make the noise
of trumpet-vine blooms. Her beams
create both the roil of sugar ants
boiling from their hill,
and the sweetness to feed them.

She is crown and halo.
Eye of All.

Give us, who once worshipped her,
a glimmer of wisdom, the gleam
of steady restraint. Let her fierceness
be shaded by her mercy,
while we attempt
the dark work of repair.

Contributors

Based in the Pacific Northwest, **HEIDI BEIERLE** works as a community planner specializing in bicycle tourism and active travel options. Her creative work has appeared in *High Desert Journal, VoiceCatcher, Journal for America's Byways,* and other publications. Her short essay, "Carnage," was nominated for a Pushcart Prize.

BESS BACALL is an Oregon writer.

ELEANOR BERRY lives in rural western Oregon. She has two full-length poetry collections, *Green November* (Traprock Books, 2007) and *No Constant Hues* (Turnstone Books of Oregon, 2015). A former college teacher of English, she is President Emerita of the National Federation of State Poetry Societies and the Oregon Poetry Association.

JOHN BRANTINGHAM is the author of seven books including *The Green of Sunset.* He teaches English at Mt. San Antonio College. In the summer he teaches free week-long poetry classes in Sequoia and Kings Canyon National Park. This piece is part of a larger memoir about living off grid.

KAMALA BREMER has received a Kay Snow award and a Fishtrap fellowship for fiction. Her essays have been published by *PorkBelly Press, VoiceCatcher,* and *Terrain.org.* Living in Portland, Oregon, she helps community service organizations chart their course for the future. Love of the outdoors and the wild inspire her life.

JEREMY CANTOR, author of *Wisteria from Seed* (Kelsay Books, 2015), was a semi-finalist for the Dartmouth Poet in Residence at The Frost Place, a finalist for the Lascaux Prize, and winner of *Grey Sparrow's* Poetry and Flash competition. He began writing after retiring from a career in laboratory chemistry.

RACHAEL DUKE lives on a probably extinct volcano in Portland, Oregon. She is a mother and aunt, the executive director of a small but mighty non-profit that develops affordable housing, and a guitar player. She writes primarily for friends and family but has two short stories published in anthologies.

JILL ELLIOTT has been published in *The Sun, The Ink-Filled Page, Where the Roses Smell the Best,* and on-line in the Literary Kitchen. Her essay "Robins" was included in the ten-year anthology of *VoiceCatcher.* She has recently completed her first novel, *Never Turn Your Back on the Ocean.*

MARE HAKE is an atypical wife and a mother to three very unalike individuals. Although she considers herself a writer, poet, and photographer, complete with a shiny MFA degree and with recent work appearing in *Terrain.org,* her most appreciated skill set still includes exercising the dog in the cold rain.

SUZY HARRIS has lived her adult life in Portland, Oregon as a teacher, attorney, life partner, parent, friend, neighbor, and writer of poems. She has been or will soon be published in *VoiceCatcher, Windfall*, Poeming Pigeon's *Poems from the Garden*, and *Calyx*. She has studied with poet Claudia Savage.

SONYA HUBER is the author of five books, including *Opa Nobody, Cover Me: A Health Insurance Memoir*, and the new essay collection *Pain Woman Takes Your Keys and Other Essays from a Nervous System*. She teaches at Fairfield University, where she directs the low-residency MFA program.

MARIA JAMES-THIAW is a performance poet and a Professor of Writing. She is the author of three books of poetry and has poems and reviews in *New Letters, Cutthroat Journal of the Arts, Black Lives Always Mattered*, and others journals and anthologies. She also coordinates the American Griot Project, where oral history meets choreo-poetry, and is completing a chapbook entitled *Mocha Musings*.

MARILYN JOHNSTON lives in Salem, Oregon. Her work is included in such literary journals as *Calyx, Natural Bridge, Poetica*, and *War, Literature and the Arts*. She received an Oregon Literary Arts Fellowship, the Donna J. Stone National Literary Award for Poetry, and the 2017 Salmon Creek Literary Journal Award for Flash Fiction.

DIANE JOSEFOWICZ's short fiction and essays have appeared in *Conjunctions, Fence, Dame Magazine, Art New England, Poets*

& Writers, and other national and regional publications. She lives in Providence, RI, with her family.

KALI LIGHTFOOT's poems have been in journals including *Illuminations 29* and *Split Rock Review*, and in the anthology *The Wildest Peal*. Her reviews of poetry books have appeared in *Bookslut* and *Green Mountains Review*. Kali has an MFA in Writing from Vermont College of Fine Arts.

ANNIE LIGHTHART started writing poetry after her first visit to an Oregon old-growth forest. Poems from her book *Iron String* have been read on *The Writer's Almanac*, turned into choral music, used in healing projects in Ireland and New Zealand, and have traveled farther than she has. www.annielighthart. com.

LOIS RUSKAI MELINA's work is forthcoming or has appeared in *Blood Orange Review, Carolina Quarterly, Colorado Review, Lunch Ticket, Chattahoochee Review,* and *2016 Best of the Net Anthology,* among others. She is retired from teaching in higher education and when not writing can sometimes be found rowing on the Willamette River near her home in Portland, Oregon.

ALISON TOWLE MOORE spent the first half of life working in nonprofits, local government and philanthropy. She then earned an MFA in Writing. She lives in Portland, Oregon with her husband where she uses writing to explore how we think, behave and evolve.

DAVID OATES writes about nature and urban life. He is author of two books of poetry and five of nonfiction, including *Paradise Wild: Reimagining American Nature*. His award-winning essays appear often in the U.S. and in the German literary journal *Wortschau*. He leads the Wild Writers Seminars in Portland, Oregon.

PAULANN PETERSEN, Oregon Poet Laureate Emerita, has six books of poetry, most recently *Understory*, from Lost Horse Press. The Latvian composer Eriks Esenvalds chose one of her poems as the lyric for a new choral composition that's now part of the repertoire of the Choir at Trinity College Cambridge.

ANDY SMART lives and works in St. Louis, Missouri. His essays have appeared in the anthology *Show Me All Your Scars* (In Fact Books, 2016) and *Green Fuse*. Andy is hopeful that the arts will survive the current sociopolitical landscape and ultimately be a force for change.

LEAH STENSON is the author of *Heavenly Body*, *The Turquoise Bee and Other Love Poems*, and *Everywhere I Find Myself* (WordTech Communications, in press). She is coeditor of two anthologies: *Alive at the Center* and *Reverberations from Fukushima*. She serves on the board of Tavern Books and hosts the Studio Series, a monthly poetry reading and open mic.

TINA TAU is a writer, artist and teacher in Portland, Oregon. She loves to go on adventures, and recently sailed across the Atlantic in a tall ship. Her work has appeared in *Calyx*, *The*

Oregonian, Wilderness Magazine, Friends Journal, and other publications. tinatau.com.

SETH MICHAEL WHITE finds inspiration for his writing and work as a river ecologist in the watery landscapes of the Pacific Northwest and Central Europe. He currently lives in Portland, Oregon, with his wife and daughters.

EDWARD WOLF writes about resilience and sustainability. His books on Pacific Northwest topics include *Klamath Heartlands* (Ecotrust, 2004), *Salmon Nation* (Ecotrust, 1999), and *A Tidewater Place* (Mountaineers Books, 1993). A graduate of Williams College and the University of Washington, he lives with his wife in Portland, Oregon.

Acknowledgments

Lois Ruskai Melina, "The Verb Forms of Aging":
appeared in *Crack the Spine* literary magazine Issue 219 (June 2016).

David Oates, "Introduction":
appeared in a different form in *Tiferet: Journal of Literature and Spirituality* (summer 2017) , and *Wortschau* (Düsseldorf, summer 2017) in German and English.

Seth Michael White, "Prelude to Catherine Creek":
appeared in *Terrain.org: Journal of the Built and Natural Environments* (2 June 2017).

CPSIA information can be obtained
at www.ICGtesting.com
Printed in the USA
FSOW02n0945220917
38821FS